JUMP Math 4.1

Book 4 Part 1 of 2

Contents

Patterns and Algebra 1	1
Number Sense 1	22
Measurement 1	97
Probability and Data Management 1	132
Geometry 1	148

jump math™

MULTIPLYING POTENTIAL.

JUMP Math
Toronto, Ontario
www.jumpmath.org

Writers: Dr. John Mighton, Dr. Sindi Sabourin, Dr. Anna Klebanov
Consultant: Jennifer Wyatt
Cover Design: Blakeley Words+Pictures
Special thanks to the design and layout team.
Cover Photograph: © LuckyOliver.com

ISBN: 978-1-897120-71-2

Permission to reprint the following images is gratefully acknowledged: pp. 86 and 97: Coin designs © courtesy of the Royal Canadian Mint / Image des pièces © courtoisie de la Monnaie royale canadienne.

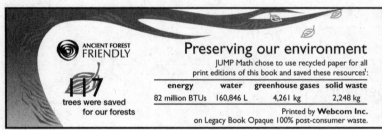

ANCIENT FOREST FRIENDLY

417

trees were saved
for our forests

Preserving our environment

JUMP Math chose to use recycled paper for all print editions of this book and saved these resources[1]:

energy	water	greenhouse gases	solid waste
82 million BTUs	160,846 L	4,261 kg	2,248 kg

Printed by **Webcom Inc.**
on Legacy Book Opaque 100% post-consumer waste.

FSC
Recycled
Supporting responsible
use of forest resources

Cert no. SW-COC-002358
www.fsc.org
© 1996 Forest Stewardship Council

[1]Estimates were made using the Environmental Defense Paper Calculator.

Printed and bound in Canada

Welcome to JUMP Math

Entering the world of JUMP Math means believing that every child has the capacity to be fully numerate and to love math. Founder and mathematician John Mighton has used this premise to develop his innovative teaching method. The resulting materials isolate and describe concepts so clearly and incrementally that everyone can understand them.

JUMP Math is comprised of workbooks, teacher's guides, evaluation materials, outreach programs, tutoring support through schools and community organizations, and provincial curriculum correlations. All of this is presented on the JUMP Math website: **www.jumpmath.org**.

Teacher's guides are available on the website for free use. Read the introduction to the teacher's guides before you begin using these materials. This will ensure that you understand both the philosophy and the methodology of JUMP Math. The workbooks are designed for use by children, with adult guidance. Each child will have unique needs and it is important to provide the child with the appropriate support and encouragement as he or she works through the material.

Allow children to discover the concepts on the worksheets by themselves as much as possible. Mathematical discoveries can be made in small, incremental steps. The discovery of a new step is like untangling the parts of a puzzle. It is exciting and rewarding.

Children will need to answer the questions marked with a in a notebook. Grid paper and notebooks should always be on hand for answering extra questions or when additional room for calculation is needed. Grid paper is also available in the BLM section of the Teacher's Guide.

The means "Stop! Assess understanding and explain new concepts before proceeding."

Contents

PART 1
Patterns & Algebra

PA4-1	Counting	1
PA4-2	Preparation for Increasing Sequences	3
PA4-3	Increasing Sequences	4
PA4-4	Counting Backwards	5
PA4-5	Decreasing Sequences	7
PA4-6	Increasing and Decreasing Sequences	8
PA4-7	Attributes	9
PA4-8	Repeating Patterns	11
PA4-9	Extending a Pattern Using a Rule	12
PA4-10	Identifying Pattern Rules	13
PA4-11	Introduction to T-tables	14
PA4-12	T-tables	16
PA4-13	Patterns Involving Time	19
PA4-14	Problem Solving with Patterns	21

Number Sense

NS4-1	Place Value – Ones, Tens, Hundreds and Thousands	22
NS4-2	Place Value	23
NS4-3	Writing Numbers	24
NS4-4	Representation with Base Ten Materials	26
NS4-5	Representation in Expanded Form	28
NS4-6	Representing Numbers (Review)	31
NS4-7	Comparing Numbers	32
NS4-8	Comparing and Ordering Numbers	33
NS4-9	Differences of 10, 100, and 1 000	35
NS4-10	Differences of 10, 100, and 1 000 (Advanced)	36
NS4-11	Counting by 10s, 100s and 1 000s	37
NS4-12	Comparing Numbers (Advanced)	38
NS4-13	Regrouping	39
NS4-14	Adding 2-Digit Numbers	42
NS4-15	Adding with Regrouping (or Carrying)	43
NS4-16	Adding with Money	45
NS4-17	Adding 3-Digit Numbers	46
NS4-18	Adding 4-Digit Numbers	48
NS4-19	Subtraction	50
NS4-20	Subtracting by Regrouping	52
NS4-21	Parts and Totals	56
NS4-22	Parts and Totals (Advanced)	57

NS4-23	Sums and Differences	58
NS4-24	Larger Numbers (Advanced)	59
NS4-25	Concepts in Number Sense	60
NS4-26	Arrays	61
NS4-27	Multiplication and Addition	62
NS4-28	Multiplying by Skip Counting & Adding On	64
NS4-29	Multiplying by Adding On	65
NS4-30	Multiples of 10	67
NS4-31	Advanced Arrays	68
NS4-32	Mental Math	69
NS4-33	Mental Math: Doubling	70
NS4-34	The Standard Method for Multiplication	71
NS4-35	Regrouping (Multiplication)	72
NS4-36	Multiplying a 3-Digit by a 1-Digit Number	73
NS4-37	Topics in Multiplication	74
NS4-38	Concepts in Multiplication	75
NS4-39	Rounding on a Number Line	76
NS4-40	Rounding on a Number Line (Hundreds)	78
NS4-41	Rounding on a Number Line (Thousands)	79
NS4-42	Rounding	80
NS4-43	Rounding on a Grid	82
NS4-44	Estimating Sums and Differences	83
NS4-45	Estimating	84
NS4-46	More Estimating	85
NS4-47	Counting Coins	86
NS4-48	Counting by Different Denominations	89
NS4-49	Least Number of Coins	91
NS4-50	Making Change Using Mental Math	93
NS4-51	Organized Lists	95

Measurement

ME4-1	Estimating Lengths in Centimetres	97
ME4-2	Measuring in Centimetres	98
ME4-3	Drawing and Measuring in Centimetres	99
ME4-4	Estimating in Millimetres	100
ME4-5	Millimetres and Centimetres	101
ME4-6	Comparing Centimetres and Millimetres	103
ME4-7	Centimetres and Millimetres (Advanced)	104
ME4-8	Problems and Puzzles	105
ME4-9	Metres	106
ME4-10	Metres (Advanced)	107
ME4-11	Kilometres	108
ME4-12	Kilometres and Metres	109

ME4-13	Ordering and Assigning Appropriate Units	110
ME4-14	Ordering Units – Metres and Centimetres	111
ME4-15	More Ordering & Assigning Appropriate Units	112
ME4-16	Perimeter	114
ME4-17	Exploring Perimeter	116
ME4-18	Measuring Perimeter	117
ME4-19	Telling Time (Review)	119
ME4-20	Telling Time (Half and Quarter Hours)	121
ME4-21	Telling Time in Two Ways	122
ME4-22	Telling Time (One-Minute Intervals)	123
ME4-23	Elapsed Time	125
ME4-24	Elapsed Time (Advanced)	126
ME4-25	Times of Day	127
ME4-26	The 24-Hour Clock	128
ME4-27	Time Intervals	129
ME4-28	Longer Time Intervals	130
ME4-29	Topics in Time	131

Probability & Data Management

PDM4-1	Introduction to Classifying Data	132
PDM4-2	Venn Diagrams	133
PDM4-3	Venn Diagrams (Advanced)	135
PDM4-4	Revisiting Pictographs	136
PDM4-5	Choosing a Pictograph Scale and Symbol	138
PDM4-6	Pictographs (Advanced)	139
PDM4-7	Introduction to Bar Graphs	140
PDM4-8	Choosing a Scale for a Bar Graph	142
PDM4-9	Double Bar Graphs	143
PDM4-10	Surveys	144
PDM4-11	Designing Your Own Survey	145
PDM4-12	Reading and Manipulating Found Data	147

Geometry

G4-1	Sides and Vertices of 2-D Figures	148
G4-2	Introduction to Angles	150
G4-3	Special Angles	152
G4-4	Measuring Angles	153
G4-5	Parallel Lines	156
G4-6	Quadrilaterals	158
G4-7	Properties of Shapes	159
G4-8	Special Quadrilaterals	161
G4-9	Tangrams	163

G4-10	Congruency	164
G4-11	Congruency (Advanced)	165
G4-12	Symmetry	166
G4-13	Symmetry and Paper Folding	167
G4-14	More Symmetry	168
G4-15	Triangles	169
G4-16	Comparing Shapes	170
G4-17	Sorting and Classifying Shapes	171
G4-18	Sorting and Classifying Shapes (Review)	173
G4-19	Puzzles and Problems	174

PART 2
Patterns & Algebra

PA4-15	Number Lines	175
PA4-16	Number Lines (Advanced)	176
PA4-17	Extending and Predicting Positions	177
PA4-18	Describing and Creating Patterns	180
PA4-19	Describing and Creating Patterns (Advanced)	181
PA4-20	2-Dimensional Patterns	183
PA4-21	2-Dimensional Patterns (Advanced)	185
PA4-22	Calendars	187
PA4-23	Patterns in the Two Times Tables	188
PA4-24	Patterns in the Five Times Tables	189
PA4-25	Patterns in the Eight Times Tables	190
PA4-26	Patterns in the Times Tables (Advanced)	191
PA4-27	Patterns with Increasing and Decreasing Steps	192
PA4-28	Advanced Patterns	193
PA4-29	Patterns with Larger Numbers	194
PA4-30	Introduction to Algebra	195
PA4-31	Algebra	196
PA4-32	Algebra (Advanced)	197
PA4-33	Problems and Puzzles	198

Number Sense

NS4-52	Sets	200
NS4-53	Sharing – Knowing the Number of Sets	202
NS4-54	Sharing – Knowing the Number in Each Set	203
NS4-55	Two Ways of Sharing	204
NS4-56	Division and Addition	207
NS4-57	Dividing by Skip Counting	208
NS4-58	The Two Meanings of Division	209
NS4-59	Division and Multiplication	211

NS4-60	Knowing When to Multiply or Divide (Introduction)	212
NS4-61	Knowing When to Multiply or Divide	213
NS4-62	Remainders	215
NS4-63	Finding Remainders on Number Lines	217
NS4-64	Mental Math – Division	218
NS4-65	Long Division – 2-Digit by 1-Digit	219
NS4-66	Further Division	224
NS4-67	Unit Rates	225
NS4-68	Concepts in Multiplication and Division	226
NS4-69	Systematic Search	227
NS4-70	Naming of Fractions	228
NS4-71	Equal Parts and Models of Fractions	229
NS4-72	Equal Parts of a Set	230
NS4-73	Parts and Wholes	232
NS4-74	Ordering and Comparing Fractions	233
NS4-75	More Ordering and Comparing Fractions	234
NS4-76	Parts and Wholes (Advanced)	235
NS4-77	Mixed Fractions	236
NS4-78	Improper Fractions	237
NS4-79	Mixed and Improper Fractions	238
NS4-80	Investigating Mixed & Improper Fractions	239
NS4-81	Mixed Fractions (Advanced)	241
NS4-82	Mixed and Improper Fractions (Advanced)	242
NS4-83	Equivalent Fractions	243
NS4-84	More Equivalent Fractions	244
NS4-85	Further Equivalent Fractions	245
NS4-86	Sharing and Fractions	246
NS4-87	More Sharing and Fractions	248
NS4-88	Sharing and Fractions (Advanced)	249
NS4-89	More Mixed and Improper Fractions	250
NS4-90	Adding and Subtracting Fractions (Introduction)	251
NS4-91	Fractions Review	252
NS4-92	Dollar and Cent Notation	253
NS4-93	Converting Between Dollar and Cent Notation	255
NS4-94	More Dollar and Cent Notation	256
NS4-95	Canadian Bills and Coins	257
NS4-96	Adding Money	258
NS4-97	Subtracting Money	260
NS4-98	Estimating	261
NS4-99	Decimal Tenths	263
NS4-100	Place Values (Decimals)	264
NS4-101	Decimal Hundredths	265
NS4-102	Tenths and Hundredths	266

NS4-103	Changing Tenths to Hundredths	267
NS4-104	Decimals and Money	268
NS4-105	Changing Notation: Fractions and Decimals	269
NS4-106	Decimals and Fractions Greater Than One	270
NS4-107	Decimals and Fractions on Number Lines	271
NS4-108	Comparing Fractions and Decimals	272
NS4-109	Ordering Fractions and Decimals	273
NS4-110	Adding and Subtracting Tenths	275
NS4-111	Adding Hundredths	276
NS4-112	Subtracting Hundredths	277
NS4-113	Adding and Subtracting Decimals (Review)	278
NS4-114	Differences of 0.1 and 0.01	279
NS4-115	Order and Place Value (Advanced)	280
NS4-116	Concepts in Decimals	281
NS4-117	Dividing by 10 and 100	282
NS4-118	Changing Units	283
NS4-119	Exploring Numbers	284
NS4-120	Word Problems	285

Measurement

ME4-30	Area in Square Centimetres	286
ME4-31	Area of Rectangles	287
ME4-32	Exploring Area	288
ME4-33	Area with Half Squares	289
ME4-34	Finding and Estimating Area	290
ME4-35	Comparing Area and Perimeter	291
ME4-36	Area and Perimeter	292
ME4-37	Problems and Puzzles	293
ME4-38	Volume	294
ME4-39	Volume of Rectangular Prisms	295
ME4-40	Mass	297
ME4-41	Changing Units of Mass	299
ME4-42	Problems Involving Mass	300
ME4-43	Capacity	301
ME4-44	Mass and Capacity	302
ME4-45	Temperature	303

Probability & Data Management

PDM4-13	Range and Median	304
PDM4-14	The Mean	305
PDM4-15	Stem and Leaf Plots	307
PDM4-16	Outcomes	310

PDM4-17	Even Chances	311
PDM4-18	Even, Likely and Unlikely	313
PDM4-19	Equal Likelihood	314
PDM4-20	Describing Probability	315
PDM4-21	Fair Games	317
PDM4-22	Expectation	318
PDM4-23	Problems and Puzzles	320

Geometry

G4-20	Introduction to Coordinate Systems	321
G4-21	Introduction to Slides	323
G4-22	Slides	324
G4-23	Slides (Advanced)	325
G4-24	Grids and Maps	326
G4-25	Games and Activities with Maps and Grids	329
G4-26	Reflections	330
G4-27	Reflections (Advanced)	331
G4-28	Rotations	332
G4-29	Rotations (Advanced)	333
G4-30	Building Pyramids	334
G4-31	Building Prisms	335
G4-32	Edges, Vertices, and Faces	336
G4-33	Prisms and Pyramids	338
G4-34	Prism and Pyramid Bases	339
G4-35	Properties of Pyramids and Prisms	341
G4-36	Nets	344
G4-37	Sorting 3-D Shapes	345
G4-38	Isoparametric Drawings	346
G4-39	Isometric Drawings	347
G4-40	Geometry in the World	348
G4-41	Problems and Puzzles	349

Helen finds the **difference** between 15 and 12 by counting on her fingers. She says "12" with her fist closed, then counts to 15, raising one finger at a time.

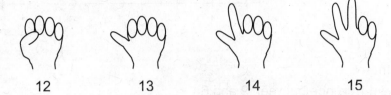

12 13 14 15

When she says "15", she has raised 3 fingers. So the difference or "gap" between 12 and 15 is 3.

- -

1. Find the difference between the numbers by counting up. Write your answer in the circle.
    (If you know your subtraction facts, you may find the answer without counting.)

a) 2   5   b) 3   8   c) 6   8   d) 4   9

e) 12   16   f) 13   17   g) 21   26   h) 37   39

i) 26   29   j) 32   37   k) 24   29   l) 44   47

m) 51   55   n) 46   49   o) 28   32   p) 34   39

q) 89   91   r) 62   71   s) 87   89   t) 59   63

BONUS:

u) 96   101   v) 79   83   w) 98   104   x) 117 122

y) 219 223   z) 146 151   aa) 99   108   bb) 99   107

TEACHER:
To help your students recognize the gap between numbers, give your students daily practice with the mental math exercises provided in the Teacher's Guide.

What number added to 6 gives 9?

$6 + \boxed{?} = 9$

Anne counts 3 spaces between 6 and 9 on a number line:

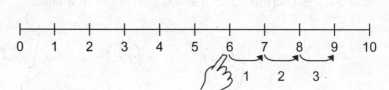

so: $6 + \boxed{3} = 9$

and: 9 is 3 **more than** 6

and: 3 is called the **difference** between 9 and 6

----

2. Use the number line (or count up) to find the <u>difference</u> between the numbers.

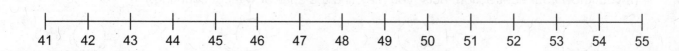

a) 42 ◯ 45   b) 43 ◯ 47   c) 51 ◯ 54   d) 44 ◯ 51

e) 42 ◯ 44   f) 49 ◯ 53   g) 47 ◯ 48   h) 45 ◯ 49

3. Use the number line (or count up) to find the <u>difference</u> between the numbers.

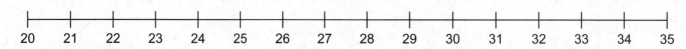

a) $23 + \boxed{2} = 25$ b) $22 + \boxed{} = 26$ c) $24 + \boxed{} = 27$

d) $\boxed{} + 22 = 24$ e) $23 + \boxed{} = 30$ f) $\boxed{} + 28 = 31$

BONUS:

4. Fill in the missing number.

a) 25 is _____ more than 23   b) 30 is _____ more than 27   c) 53 is _____ more than 46

d) 32 is _____ more than 29   e) 28 is _____ more than 25   f) 26 is _____ more than 25

g) 50 is _____ more than 49   h) 47 is _____ more than 43   i) 53 is _____ more than 48

PA4-2: Preparation for Increasing Sequences

What number is 4 **more** than 16? (Or: What is 16 + 4?)

Alissa finds the answer by counting on her fingers. She says 16 with her fist closed, then counts up from 16 until she has raised 4 fingers.

16   17   18   19   20

The number 20 is 4 **more** than 16.

----

1. Add the number in the circle to the number beside it. Write your answer in the blank.

   a) 5 ④ _____   b) 8 ② _____   c) 7 ③ _____   d) 3 ④ _____

   e) 17 ⑤ _____   f) 18 ④ _____   g) 14 ⑧ _____   h) 19 ⑥ _____

   i) 30 ⑧ _____   j) 27 ⑨ _____   k) 34 ⑦ _____   l) 32 ⑤ _____

   BONUS:

   m) 67 ② _____   n) 85 ⑤ _____   o) 42 ③ _____   p) 68 ④ _____

   q) 54 ⑥ _____   r) 63 ⑤ _____   s) 98 ④ _____   t) 93 ⑧ _____

2. Fill in the missing numbers.

   a) _____ is 4 more than 6   b) _____ is 6 more than 5   c) _____ is 5 more than 7

   d) _____ is 1 more than 19   e) _____ is 6 more than 34   f) _____ is 5 more than 18

   g) _____ is 8 more than 29   h) _____ is 7 more than 24   i) _____ is 8 more than 37

Patterns & Algebra 1

Angel wants to continue the number pattern: 6 , 8 , 10 , 12 , _?_

Step 1:   She finds the **difference** between the first two numbers.

Step 2:   She checks that the difference between the other numbers
in the pattern is also 2.

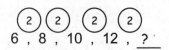

Step 3:   To continue the pattern, Angel adds 2 to the last number
in the sequence.

6 , 8 , 10 , 12 , 14

- -

1.   Extend the following patterns. Start by finding the gap between the numbers.

a)   1 , 3 , 5 , ___ , ___ , ___   b)   0 , 2 , 4 , ___ , ___ , ___

c)   3 , 7 , 11 , ___ , ___ , ___   d)   2 , 6 , 10 , ___ , ___ , ___

e)   1 , 4 , 7 , ___ , ___ , ___   f)   5 , 9 , 13 , ___ , ___ , ___

BONUS:

g)   1 , 11 , 21 , ___ , ___ , ___   h)   5 , 12 , 19 , ___ , ___ , ___

i)   21 , 24 , 27 , ___ , ___ , ___   j)   86 , 88 , 90 , ___ , ___ , ___

Use increasing sequences to solve these problems.

2.   Mary reads 5 pages of her book each night. Last night she was on page 72.

What page will she reach tonight? _____ And tomorrow night? _____

3.   Jane runs 12 blocks on Monday. Each day she runs 4 blocks further than the day before.

How far does she run on Tuesday? _____ And on Wednesday? _____

On what day of the week will she run 28 blocks? _____

PA4-4: Counting Backwards

What number must you subtract from 22 to get 18?

Dana finds the answer by counting backwards on her fingers. She uses the number line to help.

Dana has raised 4 fingers. So 4 subtracted from 22 gives 18.

- -

1. What number must you <u>subtract</u> from the greater number to get the lesser number?

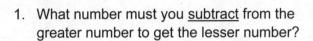

a) 23 (−3) 20   b) 24 ◯ 19   c) 21 ◯ 16   d) 22 ◯ 15

e) 24 ◯ 17   f) 19 ◯ 16   g) 23 ◯ 17   h) 25 ◯ 19

2. Find the gap between the numbers by counting backwards on your fingers.

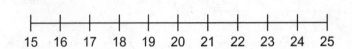

a) 42 (−4) 38   b) 41 ◯ 39   c) 42 ◯ 37   d) 38 ◯ 37

e) 41 ◯ 37   f) 40 ◯ 36   g) 42 ◯ 35   h) 43 ◯ 35

3. Find the gap between the numbers by counting backwards on your fingers (or by using your subtraction facts).

a) 86 ◯ 81   b) 58 ◯ 52   c) 50 ◯ 48   d) 80 ◯ 78

e) 52 ◯ 47   f) 67 ◯ 63   g) 45 ◯ 36   h) 62 ◯ 56

i) 58 ◯ 51   j) 101 ◯ 97   k) 82 ◯ 76   l) 97 ◯ 89

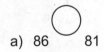
jump math
MULTIPLYING POTENTIAL

Patterns & Algebra 1

What number **subtracted** from 8 gives 5?

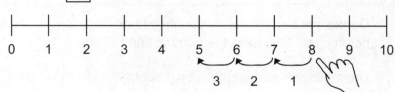

Rita puts her finger on 8 on a **number line**:

She counts (backward 3 spaces to 5)
to find the number of spaces between 8 and 5.

so: $8 - \boxed{3} = 5$ and: 5 is 3 **less than** 8

----

4. Use the number line to find the difference between the two numbers. Write your answer in the box.

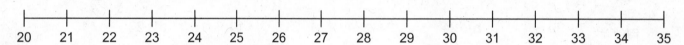

a) $27 - \square = 24$

b) $26 - \square = 23$

c) $29 - \square = 27$

d) $25 - \square = 21$

e) $28 - \square = 24$

f) $30 - \square = 25$

g) $32 - \square = 29$

h) $35 - \square = 34$

i) $30 - \square = 24$

5. What number must you <u>subtract</u> from the bigger number to get the smaller number?

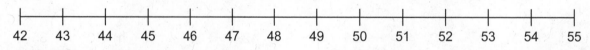

a) 47 ⟋-3⟍ 44

b) 45 ◯ 43

c) 51 ◯ 48

d) 54 ◯ 43

e) 48 ◯ 41

f) 49 ◯ 44

g) 54 ◯ 47

h) 52 ◯ 43

BONUS:

6. Fill in the missing number.

a) 47 is ____ less than 50

b) 51 is ____ less than 55

c) 46 is ____ less than 51

d) 49 is ____ less than 51

e) 48 is ____ less than 54

f) 45 is ____ less than 52

g) 44 is ____ less than 49

h) 43 is ____ less than 51

i) 52 is ____ less than 55

PA4-5: Decreasing Sequences

In a **decreasing sequence**, each number is one less than the one before it.
What number is 3 less than 9?   (Or: What is 9 – 3?)

Keitha finds the answer by counting on her fingers.
She says 9 with her fist closed and counts backwards
until she has raised 3 fingers:

9   8   7   6

The number 6 is 3 **less than** 9.

---

1. Subtract the number in the circle from the number beside it. Write your answer in the blank.

a) 3 ⊘(-2) _____   b) 12 (-3) _____   c) 8 (-4) _____   d) 9 (-1) _____

e) 8 (-5) _____   f) 10 (-4) _____   g) 5 (-1) _____   h) 9 (-2) _____

BONUS:

i) 28 (-4) _____   j) 35 (-6) _____   k) 57 (-8) _____   l) 62 (-4) _____

2. Fill in the missing numbers.

a) _____ is 4 less than 7   b) _____ is 2 less than 9   c) _____ is 3 less than 8

d) _____ is 5 less than 17   e) _____ is 4 less than 20   f) _____ is 6 less than 25

g) _____ is 7 less than 28   h) _____ is 4 less than 32   i) _____ is 5 less than 40

3. Extend the following <u>decreasing</u> patterns.

Example:

○ ○ ○ ○ ○
11 , 9 , 7 , ____ , ____ , ____

Step 1:

(-2) (-2) (-2) (-2) (-2)
11 , 9 , 7 , ____ , ____ , ____

Step 2:

(-2) (-2) (-2) (-2) (-2)
11 , 9 , 7 , 5 , 3 , 1

a) 10 , 9 , 8 , ____ , ____ , ____

b) 14 , 12 , 10 , ____ , ____ , ____

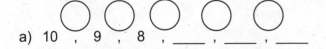
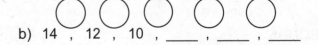

c) 23 , 22 , 21 , ____ , ____ , ____

d) 24 , 21 , 18 , ____ , ____ , ____

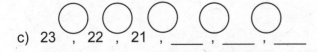
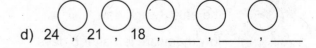

e) 90 , 80 , 70 , ____ , ____ , ____

f) 45 , 40 , 35 , ____ , ____ , ____

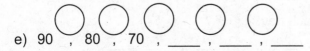

1. Extend the patterns, using the "gap" provided.

Example 1:

(+ 1)

6 , 7 , _8_ , _9_

Example 2:

(− 2)

8 , 6 , _4_ , _2_

(+ 5)

a) 5 , 10 , ___ , ___ , ___

(+ 3)

b) 1 , 4 , ___ , ___ , ___

(+ 3)

c) 3 , 6 , ___ , ___ , ___

(+ 2)

d) 6 , 8 , ___ , ___ , ___

(+ 2)

e) 12 , 14 , ___ , ___ , ___

(+ 5)

f) 10 , 15 , ___ , ___ , ___

(− 1)

g) 14 , 13 , ___ , ___ , ___

(− 2)

h) 16 , 14 , ___ , ___ , ___

2. Extend the patterns by first finding the "gap".

Example:

○   ○

3 , 5 , 7 , ___

<u>Step 1:</u>

(+ 2) (+ 2)

3 , 5 , 7 , ___

<u>Step 2:</u>

(+ 2) (+ 2)

3 , 5 , 7 , _9_

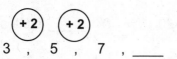

a) 5 , 8 , 11 , ___ , ___

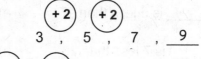

b) 2 , 4 , 6 , ___ , ___

○   ○

c) 6 , 10 , 14 , ___ , ___

○   ○

d) 1 , 3 , 5 , ___ , ___

○   ○

e) 21 , 24 , 27 , ___ , ___

○   ○

f) 12 , 17 , 22 , ___ , ___

○   ○

g) 25 , 23 , 21 , ___ , ___

○   ○

h) 59 , 54 , 49 , ___ , ___

BONUS:

3. Rachel has a box of 24 pears.

She eats 3 each day.

How many are left after 5 days? _____

4. Emi has saved $17. She saves an additional $4 each day.

How much money has she saved after 4 days? _____

Cathy is making patterns. She uses 4 different 2-D **shapes**:

circle

triangle

square

pentagon

She uses 3 **colours**: red = R
yellow = Y
blue = B

She uses 2 different **sizes**:

big   small

SHAPE, *COLOUR* and *SIZE* are referred to as the shapes' **attributes**.

TEACHER:
Make sure your students understand that while the two circles above are different sizes, they are still the same shape.

1. Circle the <u>one</u> attribute that changes in each pattern.
    HINT: Check each attribute one at a time. First ask: "Does the <u>shape</u> change?" Then ask: "Does the <u>colour</u> change?" Then ask: "Does the <u>size</u> change?"

a)

shape   colour   size

b)

shape   colour   size

c)
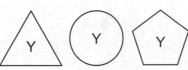
shape   colour   size

d)
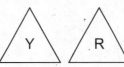
shape   colour   size

e)

shape   colour   size

f)

shape   colour   size

2. Write the <u>one</u> attribute that changes in each pattern.

a)
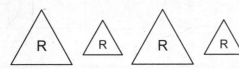
_____

b)

_____

c)

_____

d)

_____

3. Circle the <u>two</u> attributes that change in each sequence.

a)

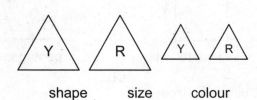

shape   size   colour

b)

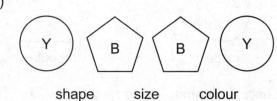

shape   size   colour

c)

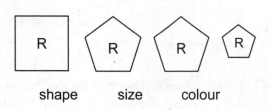

shape   size   colour

d)

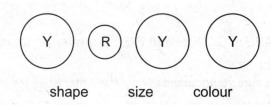

shape   size   colour

4. Write the <u>two</u> attributes that change in each pattern.

a)

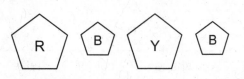

_____

b)

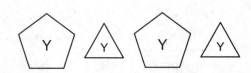

_____

c)

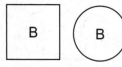 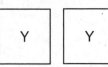

_____

d)

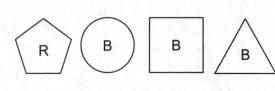

_____

5. Write the <u>one</u>, <u>two</u> or <u>three</u> attributes that change in each sequence.

a)

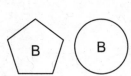

_____

b)

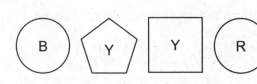

_____

c)

_____

d)

_____

PA4-8: Repeating Patterns

Marco makes a **repeating** pattern using blocks:

This is the **core** of Marco's pattern.

The **core** of a pattern is the part that repeats.

----

1. Circle the core of the following patterns. The first one is done for you.

a) 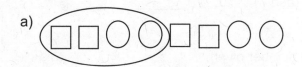   b)

c)    d)

e)    f)

g)    h) C B B C B B C B B

i) 1 2 4 1 2 4 1 2 4   j) 9 8 7 8 9 8 7 8 9 8 7 8

k) 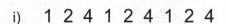   l) X Y Z X Y Z X Y Z

2. Circle the core of the pattern. Then continue the pattern.

a)  ___ ___ ___ ___ ___

b) 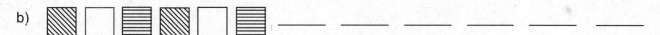 ___ ___ ___ ___ ___

c) A B C A B C A ___ ___ ___ ___

d) A B A A B A ___ ___ ___ ___ ___

e) 3 0 0 4 3 0 0 4 ___ ___ ___ ___

f) 1 8 1 1 8 1 1 8 1 ___ ___ ___ ___

jump math
MULTIPLYING POTENTIAL.

Patterns & Algebra 1

1. Continue the following sequences by <u>adding</u> the number given.

   a) (add 3)   31, 34, _____, _____, _____   b) (add 5)   70, 75, _____, _____, _____

   c) (add 2)   24, 26, _____, _____, _____   d) (add 10)   50, 60, _____, _____, _____

   e) (add 4)   31, 35, _____, _____, _____   f) (add 9)   11, 20, _____, _____, _____

   g) (add 6)   10, 16, _____, _____, _____   h) (add 7)   70, 77, _____, _____, _____

2. Continue the following sequences, <u>subtracting</u> by the number given.

   a) (subtract 2)   14, 12, ___, ___, ___   b) (subtract 3)   15, 12, ___, ___, ___

   c) (subtract 5)   75, 70, ___, ___, ___   d) (subtract 3)   66, 63, ___, ___, ___

   e) (subtract 4)   46, 42, ___, ___, ___   f) (subtract 7)   49, 42, ___, ___, ___

   g) (subtract 3)   91, 88, ___, ___, ___   h) (subtract 5)   131, 126, _____, _____, _____

BONUS:

3. Create a pattern of your own. After writing down the pattern in the blanks, give the rule you used.

   _____ , _____ , _____ , _____ , _____   My rule: _____

4. Which one of the following sequences was made by adding 3? Circle it.
   HINT: Check all the numbers in the sequence.

   a) 3, 5, 9, 12   b) 3, 6, 8, 12   c) 3, 6, 9, 12

5.   **72, 64, 56, 48, 40...**

   Zannat says this sequence was made by subtracting 7 each time.
   Faruq says it was made by subtracting 8.
   Who is right? Explain.

   _____

   _____

   _____

1. What number was added each time to make the pattern?

   a) 2, 5, 8, 11   add ____

   b) 3, 6, 9, 12   add ____

   c) 15, 17, 19, 21   add ____

   d) 44, 46, 48, 50   add ____

   e) 41, 46, 51, 56   add ____

   f) 19, 22, 25, 28   add ____

   g) 243, 245, 247, 249   add ____

   h) 21, 27, 33, 39   add ____

   i) 15, 18, 21, 24   add ____

   j) 41, 45, 49, 53   add ____

2. What number was subtracted each time to make the pattern?

   a) 18, 16, 14, 12   subtract ____

   b) 35, 30, 25, 20   subtract ____

   c) 100, 99, 98, 97   subtract ____

   d) 41, 38, 35, 32   subtract ____

   e) 17, 14, 11, 8   subtract ____

   f) 99, 97, 95, 93   subtract ____

   g) 180, 170, 160, 150   subtract ____

   h) 100, 95, 90, 85   subtract ____

   i) 27, 25, 23, 21   subtract ____

   j) 90, 84, 78, 72   subtract ____

3. State the rule for the following patterns.

   a) 119, 112, 105, 98, 91   subtract ____

   b) 1, 9, 17, 25, 33, 41   add ____

   c) 101, 105, 109, 113 _____

   d) 110, 99, 88, 77, _____

4. Find the rule for the pattern. Then continue the pattern by filling in the blanks.

   12, 17, 22, ____, ____, ____   The rule is: _____

5.   **5, 8, 11, 14, 17...**

   Keith says the pattern rule is: "Start at 5 and subtract 3 each time."
   Jane says the rule is: "Add 4 each time."
   Molly says the rule is: "Start at 5 and add 3 each time."

   a) Whose rule is correct? _____

   b) What mistakes did the others make?_____

   _____

Abdul makes a **growing pattern** with blocks.

He records the number of blocks in each figure in a chart or T-table. He also records the number of blocks he adds each time he makes a new figure.

Figure 1   Figure 2   Figure 3

Figure	# of Blocks
1	3
2	5
3	7

② Number of blocks
② added each time

The number of blocks in the figures are 3, 5, 7, …

Abdul writes a rule for this number pattern.

RULE: Start at 3 and add 2 each time.

---

1. Abdul makes other growing patterns with blocks. How many blocks does he add to make each new figure? Write your answer in the circles provided. Then write a rule for the pattern.

a)

Figure	Number of Blocks
1	3
2	7
3	11

Rule:

b)

Figure	Number of Blocks
1	2
2	6
3	10

Rule:

c)

Figure	Number of Blocks
1	2
2	4
3	6

Rule:

d)

Figure	Number of Blocks
1	1
2	6
3	11

Rule:

e)

Figure	Number of Blocks
1	5
2	9
3	13

Rule:

f)

Figure	Number of Blocks
1	12
2	18
3	24

Rule:

g)

Figure	Number of Blocks
1	2
2	10
3	18

Rule:

h)

Figure	Number of Blocks
1	3
2	6
3	9

Rule:

i)

Figure	Number of Blocks
1	6
2	13
3	20

Rule:

BONUS

2. Extend the number pattern. How many blocks would be used in the 6th figure?

a)

Figure	Number of Blocks
1	2
2	7
3	12

b)

Figure	Number of Blocks
1	3
2	6
3	9

c)

Figure	Number of Blocks
1	3
2	8
3	13

3. Amy makes a growing pattern with blocks. After making the 3rd figure, she only has 14 blocks left. Does she have enough blocks to complete the 4th figure?

a)

Figure	Number of Blocks
1	3
2	7
3	11

YES   NO

b)

Figure	Number of Blocks
1	7
2	10
3	13

YES   NO

c)

Figure	Number of Blocks
1	1
2	5
3	9

YES   NO

4. In your notebook, make a chart to show how many squares will be needed to make the <u>fifth figure</u> in each pattern.

a)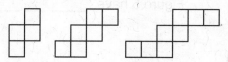

b)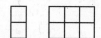

Patterns & Algebra 1

PA4-12: T-tables

1. Count the number of line segments in each set of figures.
HINT: Count around the outside of the figure first, marking each line segment as you count.

Example:

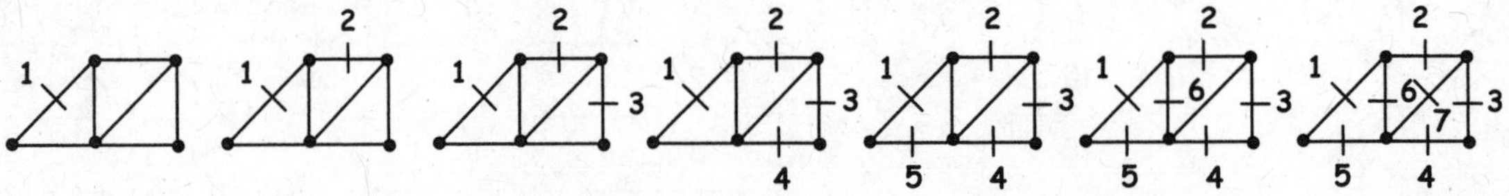

a) 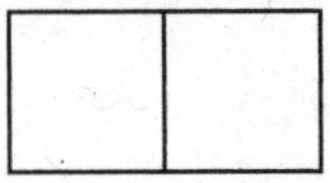 ____

b) 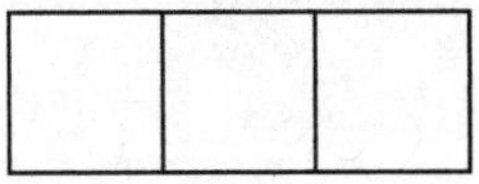 ____

c) 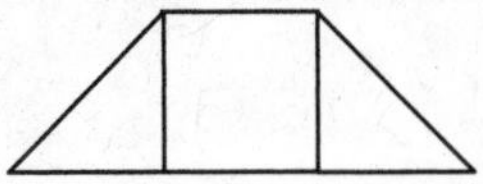 ____

d) 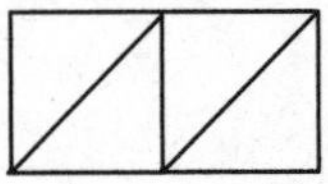 ____

e) 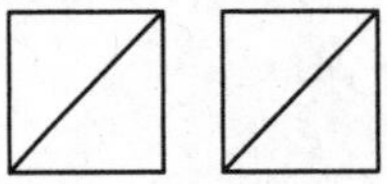 ____

f) 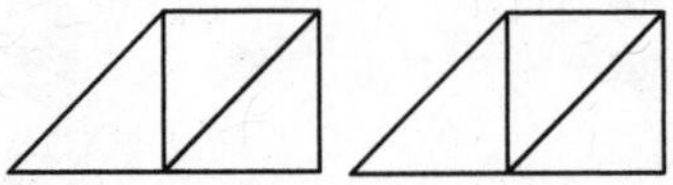 ____

2. Continue the pattern below, then complete the chart.

Figure 1

Figure 2

Figure 3

Figure 4

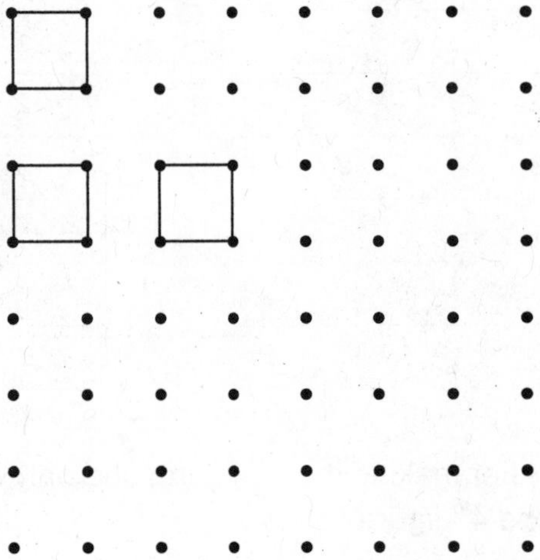

Figure	Number of Line Segments
1	4
2	8
3	
4	

How many line segments would Figure 5 have? ____________

3. Continue the pattern below, then complete the chart.

Figure 1

Figure 2

Figure 3

Figure 4

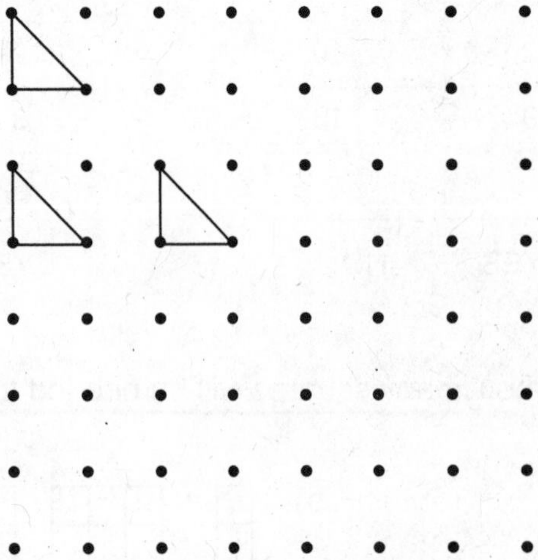

Figure	Number of Line Segments
1	
2	
3	
4	

How many line segments would Figure 5 have? ____________

PA4-12: T-tables (continued)

4. Continue the pattern below, then complete the chart.

Figure 1

Figure 2

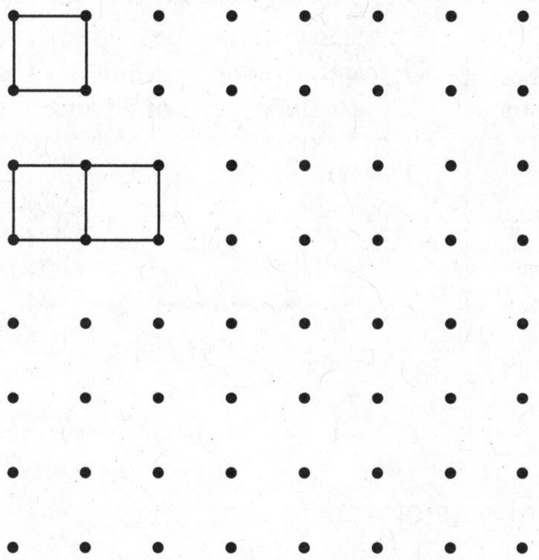

Figure 3

Figure 4

Figure	Number of Line Segments
1	
2	
3	
4	

a) How many line segments would Figure 5 have? _____

b) How many line segments would Figure 6 have? _____

c) How many line segments would Figure 7 have? _____

5. Continue the pattern below, then complete the chart.

Figure 1

Figure 2

Figure 3

Figure 4

Figure 5

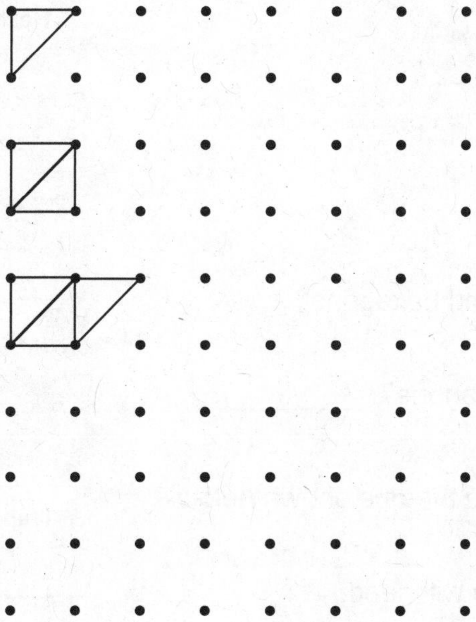

Figure	Number of Line Segments
1	
2	
3	
4	
5	

a) How many line segments would Figure 6 have? _____

b) How many line segments would Figure 7 have? _____

c) How many line segments would Figure 8 have? _____

6. Extend the chart. How many young would five animals have?

a)
Arctic Fox	Number of Cubs
1	5
2	10

b)
Wood-chuck	Number of Pups
1	4
2	8

c)
White Tailed Deer	Number of Fawns
1	2
2	4

d)
Osprey	Number of Eggs
1	3
2	6

7. How much money would Claude earn for four hours of work?

a)
Hours Worked	Dollars Earned in an Hour
1	$9

b)
Hours Worked	Dollars Earned in an Hour
1	$10

c)
Hours Worked	Dollars Earned in an Hour
1	$8

8. Step 1
   Step 2
   Step 3

Hexagons	Triangles

Peter wants to make a design using triangles and hexagons.
He has 6 hexagons and 9 triangles.

Does he have enough triangles to use all 6 hexagons? _____

9. Hanna wants to make Christmas ornaments like the one shown below.
She has 5 trapezoids (the shaded figure).

Fill in the chart to show how many triangles she will need.

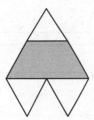

Trapezoids	Triangles

PA4-13: Patterns Involving Time

For the exercises on this page you will need to know:

The Days of the Week: **Monday, Tuesday, Wednesday, Thursday, Friday, Saturday, Sunday.**

The Months of the Year: **January, February, March, April, May, June, July, August, September, October, November, December.**

---

1. Harry starts work on Tuesday morning.
   He repairs 4 bikes each day.

Day	Total Number of Bikes Repaired
Tuesday	4

How many bikes has he repaired by Friday evening?

2. Meryl saves $20 in July.
   She saves $10 each month after that.

Month	Saved
July	$20

How much has she saved by the end of October?

3. During a snow storm, 5 cm of snow had fallen by 6 pm.
   3 cm of snow fell every hour after that.

Hour	Depth of Snow
6 pm	5 cm

How deep was the snow at 9 pm?

4. Adria's maple sapling grows 3 cm in May.
   It grows 6 cm each month after that.

Month	Height of Sapling
May	

How high is the sapling by the end of August?

5. Karen writes 14 pages of her book in February.
   She writes 8 pages every month after that.
   How many pages has she written by the end of June?

6. Mario starts work on Wednesday morning.
   He plants 5 trees each day.
   How many trees has he planted by Friday evening?

Patterns & Algebra 1

7. Sandhu lights a candle at 6 pm. It is 30 cm high.

   At 7 pm, the candle is 27 cm high.

   At 8 pm, it is 24 cm high.

   a) How many cm does the candle burn down every hour?

   Write your answers (with a minus sign) in the circles provided.

   b) How high is the candle at 11 pm?

   _____

Hour	Height of the Candle
6 pm	30 cm
7 pm	27 cm
8 pm	24 cm
9 pm	
10 pm	

8. Abdullah has $35 in his savings account at the end of March.

   He spends $7 each month.

Month	Savings
March	$35

   How much does he have in his account at the end of June?

9. Allishah has $38 in her savings account at the end of October.

   She spends $6 each month.

Month	Savings

   How much does she have at the end of January?

10. Karen has $57 in her savings account at the end of June.

    She spends $6 each month.

Month	Savings

    How much does she have at the end of September?

11. A fish tank contains 20 L of water at 5 pm.

    3 L of water leaks out each hour.

Time	Amount of Water

    How much water is left at 8 pm?

Answer the following questions in your notebook.

1. A marina rents canoes at $7 for the first hour and $4 for every hour after that. How much would it cost to rent a canoe for 6 hours?

2. A bookstore has a special sale: the first book you buy costs $10 and each book after that costs $5.
   Claude has $25.
   Does he have enough to buy five books?

3. The snow is 19 cm deep at 3 pm. 5 cm of snow falls every hour. How deep is the snow at 7 pm?

4. Jacob saves $30 in July. He saves $4 each month after that.

   Amanda saves $22 in July. She saves $6 each month after that.

   Who has saved the most money by the end of January?

5. Draw a picture or make a sequence of models (using blocks or counters) that match the pattern.

a)

Figure	Number of Objects
1	4
2	6
3	8

b)

Figure	Number of Objects
1	3
2	6
3	9

c)

Figure	Number of Objects
1	4
2	7
3	10

6. Edith's maple sapling grows 5 cm in July. It grows 7 cm each month after that.

   Ron's sapling grows 7 cm in July. It grows 3 cm each month after that.

   Whose sapling is higher by the end of September?

7. Chloe's candle is 28 cm high when she lights it at 5 pm. It burns down 4 cm every hour.

   Dora's candle is 21 cm high when she lights it at 5 pm. It burns down 3 cm every hour.

   Whose candle is taller at 10 pm?

1. Write the place value of the underlined digit.

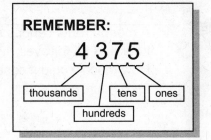

REMEMBER:

4 375

thousands   tens   ones
hundreds

a) 35<u>6</u>4 | tens | b) 1<u>3</u>36 | |

c) 25<u>6</u> | | d) <u>1</u>230 | |

e) <u>3</u>859 | | f) 5<u>7</u>45 | | g) 2<u>3</u>8 | |

h) 6<u>2</u>14 | | i) 8<u>7</u> | | j) <u>9</u>430 | |

2. Give the place value of the number 5 in each of the numbers below.
   HINT: First underline the 5 in each question.

a) 5 640 | | b) 547 | | c) 451 | |

d) 2 415 | | e) 1 257 | | f) 5 643 | |

g) 1 563 | | h) 56 | | i) 205 | |

3. You can also write numbers using a place value chart.

Example:

In a place value chart, the number 3 264 is:

thousands	hundreds	tens	ones
3	2	6	4

Write the following numbers into the place value chart.

	thousands	hundreds	tens	ones
a) 5 231	5	2	3	1
b) 8 053				
c) 489				
d) 27				
e) 9 104				
f) 4 687				

The number 2 836 is a **4-digit number**.

- The **digit** 2 stands for 2 000 – the **value** of the digit 2 is 2 000.
- The **digit** 8 stands for 800 – the **value** of the digit 8 is 800.
- The **digit** 3 stands for 30 – the **value** of the digit 3 is 30.
- The **digit** 6 stands for 6 – the **value** of the digit 6 is 6.

- -

1. Write the **value** of each digit.

a)

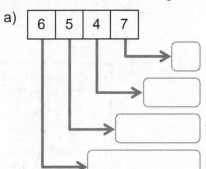

6	5	4	7

b)

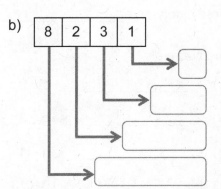

8	2	3	1

c)

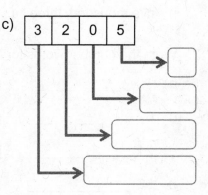

3	2	0	5

2. What does the **digit** 3 stand for in each number? The first one is done for you.

a) 237

   30

b) 5 235

c) 6 382

d) 3 280

e) 4 305

f) 6 732

g) 3 092

h) 5 883

i) 3 852

j) 1 003

k) 1 300

l) 231

3. Fill in the blanks.

   a) In the number 6 572, the <u>digit</u> 5 stands for _____ .

   b) In the number 4 236, the <u>digit</u> 3 stands for _____ .

   c) In the number 2 357, the <u>digit</u> 7 stands for _____ .

   d) In the number 8 021, the <u>value</u> of the digit 8 is _____ .

   e) In the number 6 539, the <u>value</u> of the digit 5 is _____ .

   f) In the number 3 675, the <u>value</u> of the digit 7 is _____ .

   g) In the number 1 023, the digit _____ is in the <u>tens place</u>.

   h) In the number 1 729, the digit _____ is in the <u>hundreds place</u>.

   i) In the number 7 253, the digit _____ is in the <u>thousands place</u>.

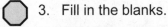

NS4-3: Writing Numbers

1. Write numerals for the number words.

   a) seven _____   b) six _____   c) eight _____

   d) twenty-three _____   e) thirty-two _____   f) ninety-five _____

   g) two hundred seventy _____   h) four hundred seventy-nine _____

   i) nine thousand, two hundred seventeen _____

   j) five thousand, three hundred ninety-one _____

Number Words for the Ones Place	
zero	five
one	six
two	seven
three	eight
four	nine

2. Write the number words for the numerals.

   a) 1 _____   b) 7 _____   c) 9 _____

   d) 6 _____   e) 2 _____   f) 3 _____

   g) 21 _____   h) 67 _____   i) 43 _____

   j) 55 _____   k) 90 _____   l) 13 _____

Number Words for the Tens Place	
ten	sixty
twenty	seventy
thirty	eighty
forty	ninety
fifty	

3. Writing numbers 100 to 9999.

   Step 1:   Underline the left-most digit. Write its value.

   a) <u>4</u> 2 5 5   <u>four thousand</u>   b) <u>2</u> 4 6   <u>two hundred</u>

   c) 3 1 6 _____   d) 7 8 2 6 _____

   e) 9 4 7 2 _____   f) 6 7 5 2 _____

   Step 2:   Cover the left-most digit. Write the number words for the remaining digits.

   g) ▮ 4 2   <u>four hundred forty-two</u>

   h) 6 9 7   <u>six hundred</u>

   i) 3 6 6 2   <u>three thousand</u>

   Complete the following number words.

   j) 4621: four thousand, __six__ hundred __twenty-one__

   k) 9876: nine thousand, _____ hundred _____

   l) 2473: two thousand, _____

   m) 1764: one thousand, _____

   n) 3502: three thousand, _____

   o) 4110: _____

NS4-3: Writing Numbers *(continued)*

4. Write number words for the following numerals.

a) 121 _____

b) 672 _____

c) 8 375 _____

d) 6 211 _____

e) 73 _____

f) 9 999 _____

5. Write the numbers provided, in words, on the signs where they are missing.

a)

(4)

_____ way

b)

House for Sale

(265)

_____

_____

Broadway Street

Enquire within.

c)

Score:

_____ points
(15)

d)

Come see the world's largest pumpkin!

_____ kg
(681)

e)

(6255)

_____ prizes available!

NS4-4: Representation with Base Ten Materials

1. Write each number in expanded form
   (numerals and words), then as a numeral.

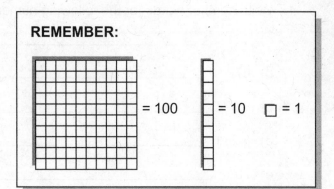
Example:

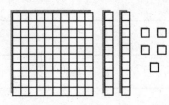

_1_ hundred + _2_ tens + _5_ ones = [125]

a)

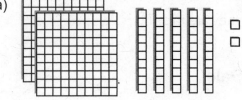

___ hundreds + ___ tens + ___ ones = [ ]

b)

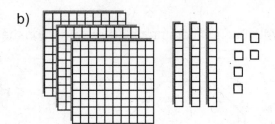

___ hundreds + ___ tens + ___ ones = [ ]

c)

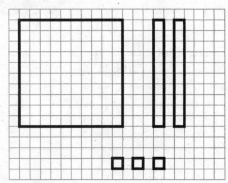

___ hundreds + ___ tens + ___ ones = [ ]

d)

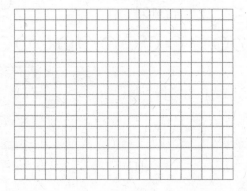

___ hundreds + ___ tens + ___ ones = [ ]

2. Using the grid paper below, draw the base ten model for the following numbers.

   a) 123   b) 132

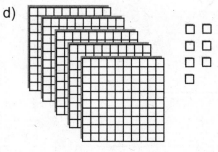

3. Draw base ten models for …   a) 68   b) 350   c) 249

Number Sense 1

4. Write each number in expanded form
   (numerals and words), then as a numeral.

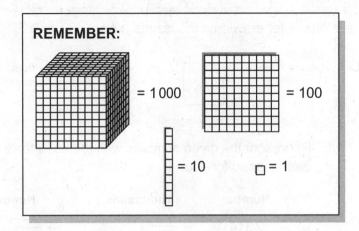

Example:

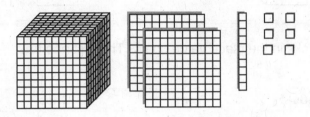

___1___ thousand + ___2___ hundreds + ___1___ tens + ___6___ ones =   [1 216]

a)

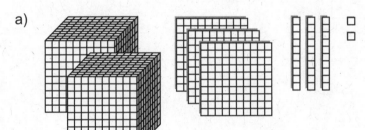

___ thousands + ___ hundreds + ___ tens + ___ ones = [   ]

b)

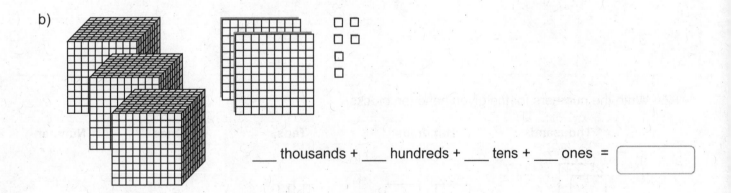

___ thousands + ___ hundreds + ___ tens + ___ ones = [   ]

c)

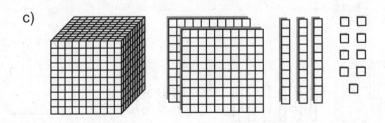

_____ = [   ]

Steps for drawing a thousands cube:

Step 1:
Draw a square.

Step 2:
Draw lines from its three vertices.

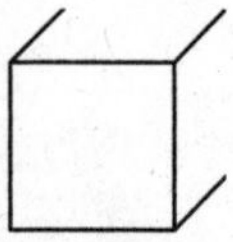

Step 3:
Join the lines.

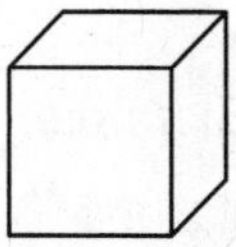

1. Represent the given numbers with the base ten blocks in the place value chart. The first one has been started for you.

	Number	Thousands	Hundreds	Tens	Ones
a)	2 314	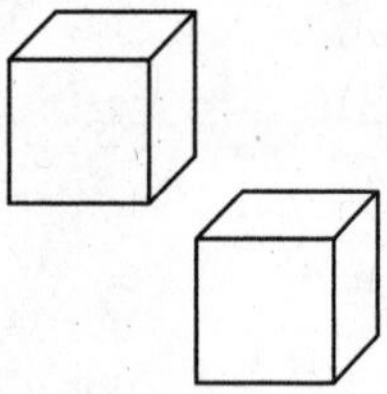	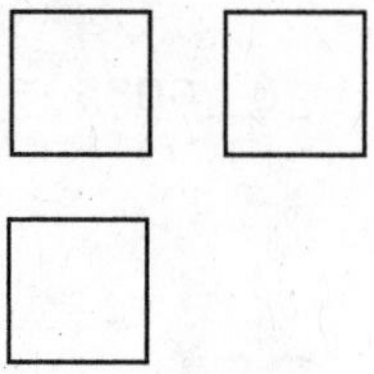		
b)	1 245				
c)	3 143				

2. Write the numbers for the given base ten blocks.

	Thousands	Hundreds	Tens	Ones	Number
a)	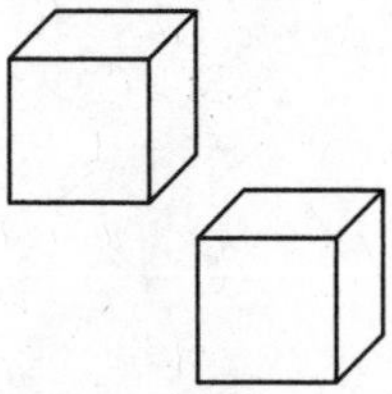	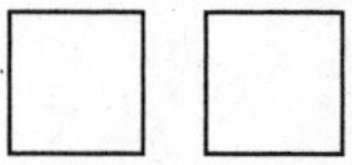	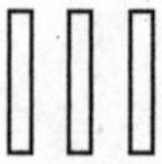	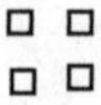	_____
b)	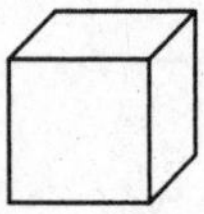	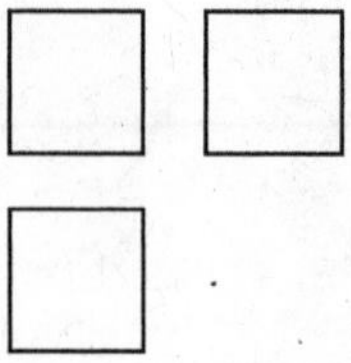	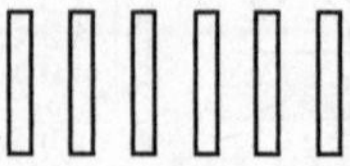	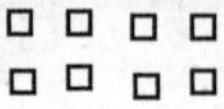	_____

3. Expand the following numbers using <u>numerals</u> and <u>words</u>. The first one is done for you.

a) 2427 = __2__ thousands + __4__ hundreds + __2__ tens + __7__ ones

b) 4569 = ____ thousands + ____ hundreds + ____ tens + ____ ones

c) 3875 = _____

d) 7210 = _____

e) 623   = _____

4. Write the number in expanded form (using <u>numerals</u>). The first one is done for you.

a) 2613 = 2000 + 600 + 10 + 3   b) 27 =

c) 48 =   d) 1232 =

e) 6103 =   f) 3570 =

g) 598 =   h) 2901 =

5. Write the number for each sum.

a) 30 + 6 =   b) 50 + 2 =   c) 60 + 5 =

d) 400 + 60 + 8 =   e) 500 + 20 + 3 =   f) 3000 + 200 + 50 + 3 =

g) 5000 + 700 + 20 + 1 = h) 600 + 40 + 5 =   i) 8000 + 900 + 70 + 2 =

BONUS

j) 600 + 7 =   k) 900 + 6 =   l) 800 + 70 =

m) 5000 + 100 =   n) 5000 + 20 =   o) 6000 + 2 =

p) 8000 + 10 + 3 =   q) 9000 + 4 =   r) 4000 + 100 + 5 =

s) 6000 + 300 + 20 =   t) 8000 + 200 =   u) 3000 + 10 =

6. Find the missing numbers.

a) 200 + 70 + _____ = 273

b) 300 + _____ + 6 = 386

c) 6 000 + 800 + _____ + 7 = 6 827

d) 1 000 + 400 + _____ + 5 = 1 475

e) 9 000 + _____ + 20 + 5 = 9 825

f) 5 000 + _____ + 60 + 3 = 5 263

BONUS

g) 7 000 + 200 + _____ = 7 202

h) 6 000 + 300 + _____ = 6 320

i) _____ + 300 = 7 300

j) 6 000 + _____ = 6 080

k) 9 000 + _____ + _____ = 9 260

l) 1 000 + _____ + _____ = 1 703

m) 7 000 + _____ + _____ = 7 021

n) 9 000 + _____ = 9 900

7. Write each number in expanded form. Then draw a base ten model.

Example: 3 213 = | 3 000 + 200 + 10 + 3

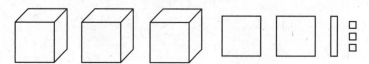

a) 2 317 = _____ + _____ + _____ + _____

b) 1 446 = _____ + _____ + _____ + _____

BONUS

8. Feliz has ...

- 1 000 stamps from Canada
- 200 stamps from Portugal
- 30 stamps from Spain
- 9 stamps from Egypt

How many stamps does he have in total? _____

Eugene makes a **model** of the number 342 using base ten materials.
He writes the number in **expanded form**, using **numerals and words** and using **numerals alone**.

342 = 3 hundreds + 4 tens + 2 ones   *expanded form (using numerals and words)*

342 = 300 + 40 + 2   *expanded form (using numerals)*

---

1. Draw a model. Write the number in expanded form using numerals and words <u>and</u> using numerals.

    a) 125

    125 = ___1 hundred + 2 tens + 5 ones_____

    125 = ___100 + 20 + 5_____

    b) 234

    234 = _____

    234 = _____

    c) 307

    307 = _____

    307 = _____

2. Write numerals for the following number words.

    a) forty-one   b) twenty-nine   c) seven hundred thirty-one

    d) one hundred ninety   e) sixty-five   f) five hundred two

    g) three hundred forty-six h) one thousand, six hundred twelve i) four thousand seven

3. Write number words for the following numbers.

    a) 952   b) 3 000   c) 4 700   d) 6 040   e) 2 981   f) 5 862

4. Represent the number 275 by sketching a model, with number words, and in expanded form.

 jump math
MULTIPLYING POTENTIAL

1. Write the number in each box. Write the name of each number on the line below. Then, circle the larger number in each pair.

   a) (i)
   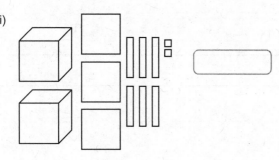

   (ii)
   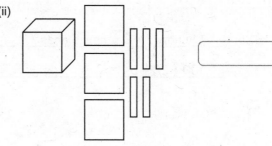

   _____

   _____

   b) (i)
   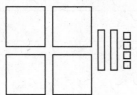

   (ii)

   _____

   _____

   _____

   _____

   c) Explain how you knew which number in part b) of Question 1 was greater.

   _____

   _____

2. Write the number in each box. Then circle the larger number in each pair.
   HINT: If there is the same number of thousands, count the number of hundreds or tens.

   a) (i)
   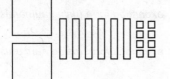

   (ii)
   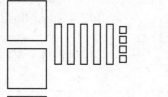

   b) (i)
   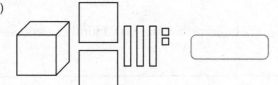

   (ii)
   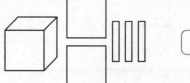

 3. Draw base ten models for the following pairs of numbers. Circle the larger number.

   a) four hundred sixteen   460

   b) one thousand three hundred   1 007

NS4-8: Comparing and Ordering Numbers

1. Write the **value** of each digit. Then complete the sentence.

a)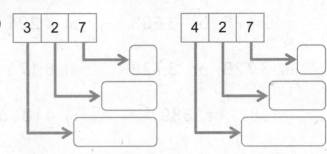

   | 8 | 7 |

   | 9 | 7 |

b)

   | 3 | 2 | 7 |

   | 4 | 2 | 7 |

_____ is greater than _____   _____ is greater than _____

2. Circle the pair of digits that are different in each pair of numbers.
   Then write the greater number in the box.

   a) 2475
      2465
      [2 475]

   b) 1360
      1260
      [   ]

   c) 4852
      4858
      [   ]

   d) 6325
      7325
      [   ]

   e) 384
      584
      [   ]

   f) 2906
      2904
      [   ]

   g) 875
      865
      [   ]

   h) 238
      231
      [   ]

3. Read the numbers from left to right.
   Circle the first pair of digits you find that are different.
   Then write the greater number in the box.

   a) 1583
      1597
      [1597]

   b) 6293
      6542
      [   ]

   c) 5769
      6034
      [   ]

   d) 9432
      9431
      [   ]

4. Read the numbers from left to right.
   Underline the first pair of digits you find that are different.
   Then circle the greater number.

   a) 2 3<u>4</u>2   (2 351)
   b) 5 201   5 275
   c) 6 327   6102

   d) 7 851   7923
   e) 5542   5540
   f) 9234   8723

   g) 3502   3501
   h) 6728   7254
   i) 2113   2145

 jump math
MULTIPLYING POTENTIAL

Number Sense 1

5. Circle the greater number.

    a) 2 175 or 3 603   b) 4 221 or 5 012   c) 6 726 or 6 591

    d) 3 728 or 3 729   e) 8 175 or 8 123   f) 5 923 or 6 000

    g) 387 or 389   h) 418 or 481   i) 2 980 or 298

6. Write < (less than) or > (greater than) in the box to make each statement true.

    a) 3 275 ☐ 4 325   b) 2 132 ☐ 2 131   c) 5 214 ☐ 5 216

    d) 528 ☐ 3 257   e) 7 171 ☐ 7 105   f) 287 ☐ 25

7. Circle the greater number in each pair.

    a) 62 or sixty-three   b) one hundred eighty-eight or 191   c) seventy-six or 71

    d) 3 725 or four thousand thirty   e) eight thousand two hundred fifty or 8 350

    f) one thousand one hundred six or 2 107   g) 6 375 or six thousand three hundred eighty-five

8. Mark each number on the number line. Then circle the greater number.

    A. 5 800   **B.** 5 700   **C.** 5 200

    5 000   6 000

9. Fill in the boxes with any digits that will make the number statements true.

    a) ☐ ☐ 7 < 3 ☐ 2   b) ☐ 2 ☐ ☐ > 5 ☐ ☐ 9

10. If you place non-zero digits in the boxes below, which number must be greater? Explain.

    ☐ 4 7   or   ☐ ☐ 2 3

11. How many whole numbers are greater than 5 900 and less than 6 000?

12. Montreal is 539 km away from Toronto. Ottawa is 399 km away. Which city is further from Toronto?

jump math
MULTIPLYING POTENTIAL.

Number Sense 1

NS4-9: Differences of 10, 100, and 1000

1. Write "10 more" or "10 less" in the blanks.

   a) 90 is _____ than 80

   b) 30 is _____ than 40

   c) 10 is _____ than 20

   d) 100 is _____ than 90

2. Write "100 more" or "100 less" in the blanks.

   a) 600 is _____ than 500

   b) 700 is _____ than 800

   c) 700 is _____ than 600

   d) 800 is _____ than 900

3. Write "1000 more" or "1000 less" in the blanks.

   a) 7000 is _____ than 6000

   b) 1000 is _____ than 2000

4. Write the value of the digits. Then say how much more or less the first number is than the second.

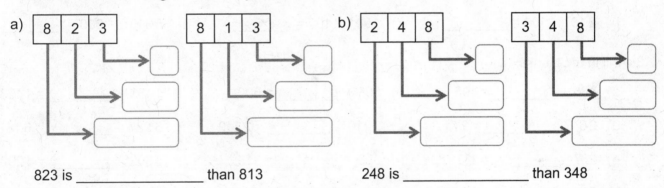

   a)

   | 8 | 2 | 3 |
   | 8 | 1 | 3 |

   823 is _____ than 813

   b)

   | 2 | 4 | 8 |
   | 3 | 4 | 8 |

   248 is _____ than 348

5. Circle the pair of digits that are different. Then fill in the blanks.

   a) 2652
      2752

      2652 is _____100 less_____ than 2752

   b) 1382
      1482

      1382 is _____ than 1482

   c) 6830
      7830

      6830 is _____ than 7830

   d) 3621
      2621

      3621 is _____ than 2621

   e) 8405
      8415

      8405 is _____ than 8415

   f) 5871
      5872

      5871 is _____ than 5872

1. Fill in the blanks.

   a) _____ is 10 more than 287   b) _____ is 10 less than 363

   c) _____ is 10 less than 1982   d) _____ is 10 more than 3603

   e) _____ is 100 more than 592   f) _____ is 100 less than 4135

   g) _____ is 100 more than 6821   h) _____ is 100 less than 3295

   i) _____ is 1000 less than 8305   j) _____ is 1000 more than 4253

2. Fill in the blanks.

   a) $743 + 10 =$ _____   b) $2382 + 10 =$ _____   c) $9035 + 10 =$ _____

   d) $1270 + 100 =$ _____   e) $1952 + 100 =$ _____   f) $8321 + 1000 =$ _____

   g) $357 - 10 =$ _____   h) $683 - 10 =$ _____   i) $932 - 100 =$ _____

   j) $2487 - 100 =$ _____   k) $1901 - 100 =$ _____   l) $5316 - 1000 =$ _____

3. Fill in the blanks.

   a) $485 +$ _____ $= 495$ b) $503 +$ _____ $= 603$ c) $1483 +$ _____ $= 1493$

   d) $2617 +$ _____ $= 2717$ e) $3210 -$ _____ $= 2210$ f) $6287 -$ _____ $= 6187$

   g) $287 -$ _____ $= 187$ h) $325 -$ _____ $= 315$ i) $4392 -$ _____ $= 4292$

   j) $7001 -$ _____ $= 6001$ k) $2301 -$ _____ $= 2201$ l) $8027 +$ _____ $= 8127$

4. Fill in the blanks.

   a) $93 + 10 =$ _____   b) $295 + 10 =$ _____   c) $394 + 10 =$ _____

   d) $2492 + 10 =$ _____   e) $5395 + 10 =$ _____   f) $8096 + 10 =$ _____

   g) $3972 + 100 =$ _____   h) $4923 + 100 =$ _____   i) $6902 + 100 =$ _____

   j) $892 +$ _____ $= 902$ k) $597 +$ _____ $= 607$ l) $7922 +$ _____ $= 8022$

   m) $301 - 10 =$ _____   n) $2507 - 10 =$ _____   o) $9397 + 10 =$ _____

BONUS
5. Continue the patterns.

   a) 508, 518, 528, _____, _____   b) 6532, 6542, 6552, _____, _____

   c) 1482, 1492, _____, 1512, _____   d) 8363, _____, _____, 8393, 8403

NS4-11: Counting by 10s, 100s and 1000s

1. Count by 10s to continue the pattern.

   a) 30, 40, 50, _____, _____, _____
   b) 10, 20, 30, _____, _____, _____

   c) 50, 60, 70, _____, _____, _____
   d) 23, 33, 43, _____, _____

   e) 27, 37, 47, _____, _____, _____
   f) 15, 25, 35, _____, _____, _____

   g) 49, 59, 69, _____, _____, _____
   h) 1, 11, 21, _____, _____

   i) 100, 110, 120, _____, _____, _____
   j) 160, 170, 180, _____, _____, _____

2. Count by 100s to continue the pattern.

   a) 100, 200, 300, _____, _____, _____
   b) 600, 700, 800, _____, _____, _____

   c) 300, 400, 500, _____, _____, _____
   d) 1 000, 1 100, 1 200, _____, _____, _____

3. There are 100 marbles in a bag. How many marbles would there be in …

   a) 2 bags? _____
   b) 4 bags? _____
   c) 5 bags? _____

4. Count by 100s to complete the pattern. The first one has been done for you.

   a) 101, 201, 301, __401__ , __501__
   b) 110, 210, 310, _____, _____

   c) 227, 327, 427, _____, _____, _____
   d) 399, 499, 599, _____, _____, _____

   e) 45, 145, 245, _____, _____, _____
   f) 525, 625, 725, _____, _____, _____

5. Count by 1000s to continue the pattern.

   a) 1 000, 2 000, _____, _____, _____
   b) 6 000, 7 000, _____, _____, _____

6. There are 1000 nails in a bag. How many nails would there be in …

   a) 3 bags? _____
   b) 4 bags? _____
   c) 5 bags? _____

7. Count down by 100s.

   a) 700, 600, 500, _____, _____, _____
   b) 1 000, 900, 800, _____, _____, _____

   c) 2200, 2100, _____, _____, _____
   d) 5 100, 5 000, _____, _____, _____

8. Count down by 1000s.

   a) 9 000, 8 000, 7 000, _____, _____
   b) 5 000, 4 000, _____, _____, _____

1. Create the greatest possible 3-digit number using the digits given (only use each digit once).

    a) 4, 3, 2 [   ]   b) 7, 8, 9 [   ]   c) 0, 4, 1 [   ]

    BONUS
    Now make the greatest 4-digit number.

    d) 5, 1, 2, 8 [   ]   e) 4, 9, 1, 5 [   ]   f) 6, 1, 5, 4 [   ]

2. Use the digits to create the greatest number, the least number and any number in between (use each digit exactly once).

	Digits	Greatest Number	Number in Between	Least Number
a)	5 7 2 1			
b)	4 9 8 6			
c)	2 7 7 5			

3. Arrange the numbers in order, starting with the least number.

    a) 175, 162, 187

    _____ , _____ , _____

    c) 3950, 3850, 3270

    _____ , _____ , _____

    e) 2023, 2027, 2100

    _____ , _____ , _____

    b) 7251, 7385, 7256

    _____ , _____ , _____

    d) 9432, 9484, 9402

    _____ , _____ , _____

    f) 4201, 4110, 4325

    _____ , _____ , _____

4. List all the 3-digit numbers you can make using the digits provided. Then circle the greatest one.
    NOTE: Only use each number once.

    a) 3, 4, and 5

    b) 6, 1, and 7

Carl has 5 tens blocks and 17 ones blocks. He regroups 10 ones as 1 tens block.

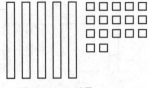

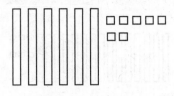

5 tens + 17 ones   =   6 tens + 7 ones

---

1. Regroup 10 ones blocks as 1 tens block.

a)

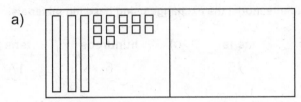

___ tens + ___ ones = ___ tens + ___ ones

b)

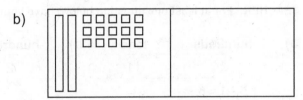

___ tens + ___ ones = ___ tens + ___ ones

c)

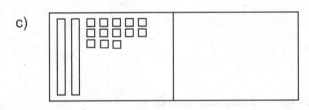

___ tens + ___ ones = ___ tens + ___ ones

d)

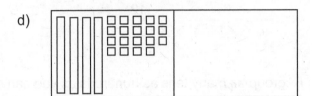

___ tens + ___ ones = ___ tens + ___ ones

2. Complete the charts by regrouping as many ones as tens as you can. The first one has been done.
    REMEMBER: 10 ones = 1 ten, 20 ones = 2 tens, 30 ones = 3 tens, and so on.

a)

tens	ones
6	25
6 + 2 = 8	5

= 85

b)

tens	ones
8	32

=

c)

tens	ones
5	31

=

d)

tens	ones
7	17

=

e)

tens	ones
6	29

=

f)

tens	ones
1	52

=

3. Regroup ones as tens.

a) 23 ones = ___ tens + ___ ones   b) 56 ones = ___ tens + ___ ones   c) 86 ones = ___ tens + ___ ones

d) 58 ones = ___ tens + ___ ones   e) 18 ones = ___ tens + ___ ones   f) 72 ones = ___ tens + ___ ones

g) 80 ones = ___ tens + ___ ones   h) 7 ones = ___ tens + ___ ones   i) 98 ones = ___ tens + ___ ones

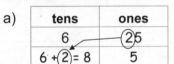

Mehmet has 2 hundreds blocks, 15 tens blocks, and 6 ones blocks. He regroups 10 tens blocks as 1 hundreds block.

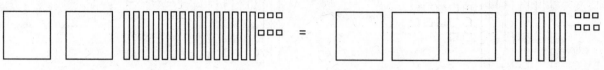

2 hundreds + 15 tens + 6 ones   3 hundreds + 5 tens + 6 ones

----

4. Complete the charts by regrouping 10 tens as 1 hundred.
    TEACHER: For at least one question below, have your students model the exchange using base ten materials.

a)

hundreds	tens
5	11
5 + 1 = 6	1

b)

hundreds	tens
2	15

c)

hundreds	tens
6	17

d)

hundreds	tens
6	12

e)

hundreds	tens
2	17

f)

hundreds	tens
5	10

5. Regroup as many tens as hundreds as you can.
    REMEMBER: 10 tens = 1 hundred, 20 tens = 2 hundreds, 30 tens = 3 hundreds and so on.

a) 3 hundreds + 13 tens + 4 ones = _____ hundreds + _____ tens + _____ ones

b) 5 hundreds + 21 tens + 1 ones = _____ hundreds + _____ tens + _____ ones

c) 3 hundreds + 10 tens + 5 ones = _____

d) 1 hundreds + 34 tens + 7 ones = _____

6. Regroup tens as hundreds or ones as tens. The first one has been done for you.

a) 4 hundreds + 2 tens + 19 ones = ___ 4 hundreds + 3 tens + 9 ones ___

b) 7 hundreds + 25 tens + 2 ones = _____

c) 2 hundreds + 43 tens + 6 ones = _____

d) 7 hundreds + 1 tens + 61 ones = _____

e) 0 hundreds + 26 tens + 3 ones = _____

Maya has 1 thousands block, 11 hundreds blocks, 1 tens block and 2 ones blocks.
She regroups 10 hundreds blocks as 1 thousands block.

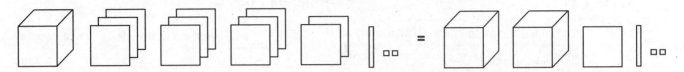

1 thousand + 11 hundreds + 1 ten + 2 ones   2 thousands + 1 hundred + 1 ten + 2 ones

---

7. Complete the charts by regrouping 10 hundreds as 1 thousand.
   TEACHER: For at least one question, have your students model the exchange using base ten materials.

a)

thousands	hundreds
3	12
3 + 1 = 4	2

b)

thousands	hundreds
4	13

c)

thousands	hundreds
7	14

8. Regroup hundreds as thousands, tens as hundreds, or ones as tens. The first one has been done.

   a) 5 thousands + 12 hundreds + 3 tens + 1 one = __6__ thousands + __2__ hundreds + __3__ tens + __1__ one

   b) 3 thousands + 15 hundreds + 1 ten + 6 ones = ____ thousands + ____ hundreds + ____ ten + ____ ones

   c) 3 thousands + 26 hundreds + 5 tens + 1 one = ____ thousands + ____ hundreds + ____ tens + ____ one

   d) 6 thousands + 14 hundreds + 6 tens + 5 ones = _____

   _____

   e) 2 thousands + 18 hundreds + 0 tens + 7 ones = _____

   _____

   f) 6 thousands + 6 hundreds + 23 tens + 5 ones = _____

   _____

9. Roger wants to build a model of three thousand, two hundred twelve.
   He has 3 thousands blocks, 1 hundreds block and 24 ones blocks.
   Can he build the model?
   Use diagrams and numbers to explain your answer.

1. Find the <u>sum</u> of the numbers below by drawing a picture and by adding the digits.
    Don't worry about drawing the model in too much detail.

a) 15 + 43

	with base ten materials		with numerals	
	tens	ones	tens	ones
15	(ten rod)	▫▫▫▫▫	1	5
43	(4 ten rods)	▫▫▫	4	3
sum	(5 ten rods)	▫▫▫▫▫ ▫▫▫	5	8

b) 25 + 22

	with base ten materials		with numerals	
	tens	ones	tens	ones
25				
22				
sum				

c) 31 + 27

	with base ten materials		with numerals	
	tens	ones	tens	ones
31				
27				
sum				

d) 13 + 24

	with base ten materials		with numerals	
	tens	ones	tens	ones
13				
24				
sum				

2. Add the numbers by adding the digits.

a) 3 4
  + 4 3

b) 7 7
  + 1 2

c) 5 4
  + 3 5

d) 1 0
  + 4 9

e) 1 6
  + 2 3

f) 1 6
  + 2 1

g) 5 2
  + 2 4

h) 8 1
  + 1 1

i) 4 3
  + 3 1

j) 7 5
  + 1 4

NS4-15: Adding with Regrouping (or Carrying)

1. Add the numbers below by drawing a picture and by adding the digits.
   Use base ten materials to show how to combine the numbers and how to regroup.

a) **16 + 25**

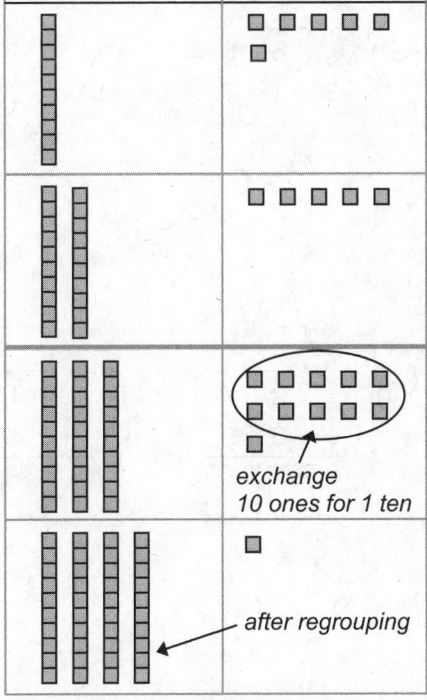

exchange
10 ones for 1 ten
after regrouping

	with base ten materials		with numerals	
	tens	ones	tens	ones
16			1	6
25			2	5
sum			3	11
			4	1

b) **25 + 37**

	with base ten materials		with numerals	
	tens	ones	tens	ones
25				
37				
sum				

c) **29 + 36**

	with base ten materials		with numerals	
	tens	ones	tens	ones
29				
36				
sum				

d) **17 + 35**

	with base ten materials		with numerals	
	tens	ones	tens	ones
17				
35				
sum				

2. Add the numbers by regrouping.

    <u>Step 1</u>:   *Regroup 10 ones as 1 ten.*

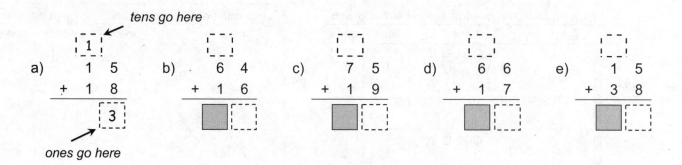

    a)   1   5   b)   6   4   c)   7   5   d)   6   6   e)   1   5
       + 1   8   +   1   6   +   1   9   +   1   7   +   3   8

    f)   1   3   g)   2   4   h)   5   4   i)   2   7   j)   4   6
       + 1   9   +   3   8   +   1   8   +   6   9   +   4   8

    <u>Step 2</u>:   *Add the numbers in the tens column.*

    k)   1   2   l)   1   3   m)   1   5   n)   2   6   o)   3   8
       + 1   8   +   1   7   +   2   8   +   2   6   +   2   7
       ───────   ──────────   ──────────   ──────────   ──────────
         3   0   0   3   2   5

3. Add the numbers by regrouping. The first one has been done for you.

    a)   1   b)   3   7   c)   5   9   d)   3   7   e)   5   7
            3   6   +   1   8   +   1   8   +   4   3   +   2   6
       + 1   8
       ───────
         5   4

    f)   6   3   g)   5   8   h)   1   8   i)   5   9   j)   7   5
       +   2   9   +   4   7   +   7   7   +   1   3   +   1   6

NS4-16: Adding with Money

1. Rewrite each amount in dimes and pennies.

a) 51¢ = __5__ dimes + __1__ penny

b) 23¢ = _____ dimes +_____ pennies

c) 67¢ = _____ dimes +_____ pennies

d) 92¢ = _____ dimes +_____ pennies

e) 84¢ = _____ dimes +_____ pennies

f) 70¢ = _____ dimes +_____ pennies

g) 2¢ = _____ dimes +_____ pennies

h) 5¢ = _____ dimes +_____ pennies

2. Show how to regroup ten pennies as 1 dime.

a)

dimes	pennies
2	12
3	2

after regrouping

b)

dimes	pennies
5	13

c)

dimes	pennies
7	17

d)

dimes	pennies
4	18

3. Find the total number of dimes and pennies. Then regroup.

a)

dimes	pennies
3	5
2	6
5	11
6	1

total after regrouping

b)

dimes	pennies
2	6
3	6

c)

dimes	pennies
5	2
2	9

d)

dimes	pennies
3	3
4	9

4. Add by regrouping 10 pennies as 1 dime.

a)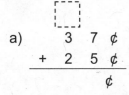
```
    3  7  ¢
 +  2  5  ¢
 _____
          ¢
```

b)
```
    2  3  ¢
 +  4  9  ¢
 _____
          ¢
```

c)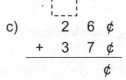
```
    2  6  ¢
 +  3  7  ¢
 _____
          ¢
```

d)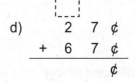
```
    2  7  ¢
 +  6  7  ¢
 _____
          ¢
```

e)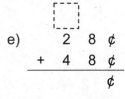
```
    2  8  ¢
 +  4  8  ¢
 _____
          ¢
```

5. Add by lining the dimes and pennies up in the gird.

a) 15¢ + 17¢   b) 23¢ + 27¢   c) 48¢ + 59¢   d) 26¢ + 34¢   e) 27¢ + 85¢

	1	5	¢															
+	1	7	¢															

NS4-17: Adding 3-Digit Numbers

Dalha adds 152 + 273 using base ten materials.

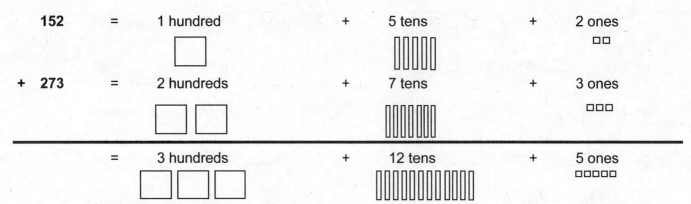

Then, to get the final answer, Dalha regroups 10 tens as 1 hundred.

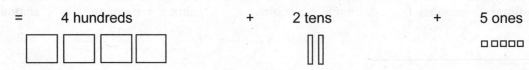

1. Add the numbers using base ten materials or a picture (and record your work below).

a)   **353**
     + 164

_____ hundreds + _____ tens + _____ ones

+ _____ hundred + _____ tens + _____ ones

= _____ hundreds + _____ tens + _____ ones

after regrouping   = _____ hundreds + _____ ten + _____ ones

b)   **462**
     + 375

_____ hundreds + _____ tens + _____ ones

+ _____ hundreds + _____ tens + _____ ones

= _____ hundreds + _____ tens + _____ ones

after regrouping   = _____ hundreds + _____ tens + _____ ones

2. Add. You will need to regroup. The first one is started for you.

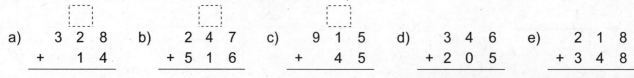

a)   1
      5 2 6
    + 2 9 3
    ———————
        1 9

b)   6 4 5
      + 1 8 3

c)   3 7 4
      + 4 6 2

d)   4 8 2
      + 4 7 7

e)   2 8 4
      + 5 9 5

3. Add. You will need to regroup ones as tens.

a)   3 2 8
      +   1 4

b)   2 4 7
      + 5 1 6

c)   9 1 5
      +   4 5

d)   3 4 6
      + 2 0 5

e)   2 1 8
      + 3 4 8

4. Add, regrouping where necessary.

a) 564
   + 153

b) 248
   + 424

c) 526
   + 348

d) 164
   + 672

e) 444
   + 209

f) 856
   + 134

5. Add by lining the numbers up correctly in the grid. The first one has been started for you.

a) 218 + 265   b) 272 + 213   c) 643 + 718   d) 937 + 25

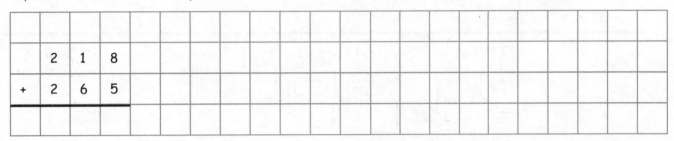

| | 2 | 1 | 8 |
| + | 2 | 6 | 5 |

e) 146 + 273   f) 816 + 925   g) 369 + 119   h) 847 + 910

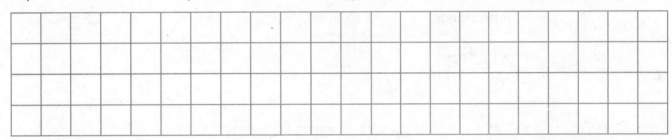

i) 387 + 203   j) 822 + 978   k) 27 + 132   l) 586 + 9

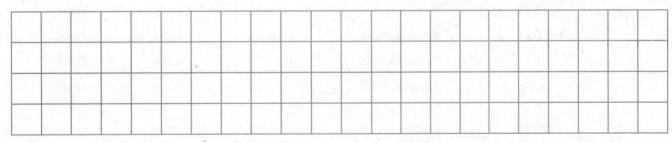

BONUS

6. Use the pattern in your answers to a), b), and c) to find the sums in d) and e) without adding.

a)   9
      + 9

b)   99
     + 99

c)   999
    + 999

d)   9999
    + 9999

e)   99999
    + 99999

7. How do you think you would add the numbers below?

a) 22 + 36 + 21   b) 324 + 112 + 422   c) 131 + 204 + 351

Amber adds 1 852 + 2 321 using base ten materials.

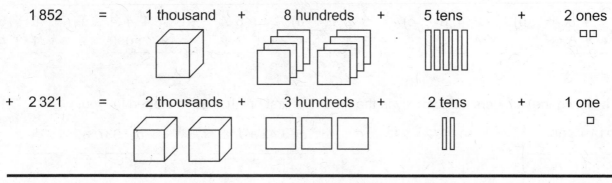

| 1 852 | = | 1 thousand | + | 8 hundreds | + | 5 tens | + | 2 ones |

| + 2 321 | = | 2 thousands | + | 3 hundreds | + | 2 tens | + | 1 one |

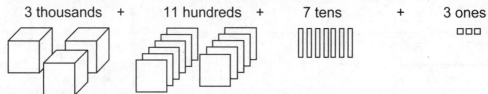

| | = | 3 thousands | + | 11 hundreds | + | 7 tens | + | 3 ones |

Then, to get the final answer, Amber regroups 10 hundreds as 1 thousand.

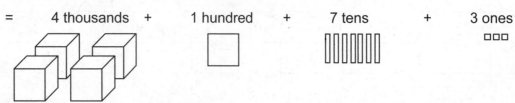

| | = | 4 thousands | + | 1 hundred | + | 7 tens | + | 3 ones |

- -

1. Add the numbers using base ten materials or a picture. Record your work below.

a)   2 543   _____ thousands + _____ hundreds + _____ tens + _____ ones

  + 3 621   + _____ thousands + _____ hundreds + _____ tens + _____ ones

            _____ thousands + _____ hundreds + _____ tens + _____ ones

after regrouping   _____ thousands + _____ hundreds + _____ tens + _____ ones

b)   3 824   _____ thousands + _____ hundreds + _____ tens + _____ ones

  + 1 654   + _____ thousands + _____ hundreds + _____ tens + _____ ones

            _____ thousands + _____ hundreds + _____ tens + _____ ones

after regrouping   _____ thousands + _____ hundreds + _____ tens + _____ ones

2. Add. (You will need to regroup.) The first one is started for you.

a) [1]
   5 2 6 5
 + 2 9 1 2
    1 7 7

b) [ ]
   6 4 5 4
 + 1 8 3 3

c) [ ]
   3 7 4 7
 + 2 6 2 1

d) [ ]
   1 8 2 1
 + 2 7 7 2

e) [ ]
   1 8 2 4
 + 5 7 7 3

3. Add. You will need to carry into the hundreds.

a)
```
      3 4 8 3
    + 1 3 3 4
```
b)
```
      2 5 6 9
    + 1 2 6 0
```
c)
```
      5 4 8 6
    + 1 1 3 1
```
d)
```
      8 3 6 4
    + 1 4 7 2
```
e)
```
      1 2 9 4
    + 5 0 9 3
```

4. Add. You will need to carry into the tens.

a)
```
      2 4 3 6
    + 1 1 2 5
```
b)
```
      8 1 2 7
    + 1 7 4 3
```
c)
```
      7 5 8 8
    + 2 1 0 8
```
d)
```
      5 4 2 5
    + 2 3 4 7
```
e)
```
      6 2 5 4
    + 2 6 3 9
```

5. Add (carrying where necessary).

a)
```
      2 3 5 4
    + 2 8 3 1
```
b)
```
      4 6 8 3
    + 1 7 4 2
```
c)
```
      3 8 3 1
    + 4 8 3 3
```
d)
```
      6 5 2 5
    + 1 5 3 3
```
e)
```
      3 8 4 4
    + 2 7 2 3
```

f)
```
      3 5 4 6
    + 4 8 2 2
```
g)
```
      7 6 2 4
    + 1 6 0 1
```
h)
```
      5 6 4 0
    + 3 7 1 2
```
i)
```
      2 9 2 5
    + 1 7 5 1
```
j)
```
      3 2 4 5
    + 3 4 3 1
```

6. Add by lining the numbers up correctly in the grid. In some questions you may have to carry twice.

a) 4 534 + 2 542   b) 6 754 + 1 360   c) 3 214 + 4 852   d) 2 509 + 621

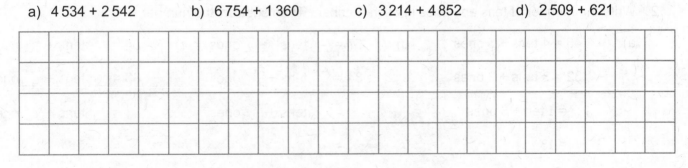

7. How do you think you might add the following numbers?

a)
```
      2 5 3 7 2
    + 6 0 5 2 1
```
b)
```
      5 3 8 2 7
    + 2 4 1 1 3
```
c)
```
      3 8 7 6 9 1
    + 1 3 4 1 2 0
```

Bradley subtracts 48 – 32 by making a model of 48.

He takes away 3 tens and 2 ones (because 32 = 3 tens + 2 ones).

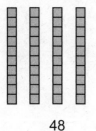 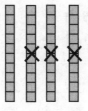 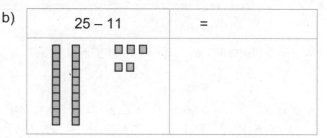 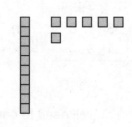

    48   48 – 32   =   16

---

1. Subtract by crossing out tens and ones blocks. Draw your final answer in the right hand box.

a)   39 – 18   = 21

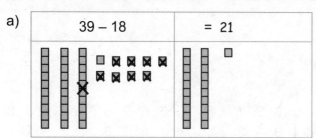

b)   25 – 11   =

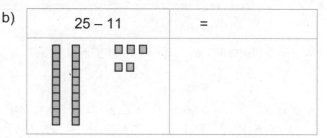

c)   43 – 21   =

d)   45 – 32   =

2. Write the number of tens and ones in each number. Then subtract the number.

a)   45 = 4 tens + 5 ones

    –   32 = 3 tens + 2 ones

        = 1 ten + 3 ones

        = 13

b)   57 = ___ tens + ___ ones

    –   34 = ___ tens + ___ ones

        = ___ tens + ___ ones

        = ____

c)   84 = ___ tens + ___ ones

    –   63 = ___ tens + ___ ones

        = ___ tens + ___ ones

        = ____

d)   89 = ___ tens + ___ ones

    –   56 = ___ tens + ___ ones

        = ___ tens + ___ ones

        = ____

e)   77 = ___ tens + ___ ones

    –   44 = ___ tens + ___ ones

        = ___ tens + ___ ones

        = ____

f)   67 = ___ tens + ___ ones

    –   45 = ___ tens + ___ ones

        = ___ tens + ___ ones

        = ____

3. Subtract by writing the number of tens and ones in each number.

    a)   36 = 30 + 6   b)   84 =   c)   98 =

         − 24 = 20 + 4   − 52 =   − 37 =
        ─────────────────   ────────────   ────────────
             = 10 + 2   =   =

             = 12   =   =

    d)   73 =   e)   26 =   f)   88 =

         − 12 =   − 24 =   − 33 =
        ─────────────────   ────────────   ────────────

4. Subtract the numbers by subtracting the digits.

    a)   5 4   b)   8 6   c)   3 6   d)   6 4   e)   9 5   f)   8 9
        − 2 3   − 7 3   − 1 5   − 3 2   − 4 2   − 4 0
        ───────   ───────   ───────   ───────   ───────   ───────

5. a) Draw a picture of 543 using hundreds, tens and ones blocks.
        Show how you would subtract 543 − 421.

    b) Now subtract the numbers by lining up the digits and subtracting. Do you get the same answer?

6. How do you think you would subtract the following numbers? Show what you think the answer
    would be.

    a)   7 5 3 2   b)   6 5 3 5 6   c)   9 5 5 7 6 3
        − 4 1 2 1   − 4 4 2 4 5   − 5 2 3 0 1 1
        ───────────   ─────────────   ───────────────

NS4-20: Subtracting by Regrouping

Farkan subtracts 46 − 18 using base ten materials.

Step 1:
Farkan represents 46 with base ten materials.

tens	ones
4	6

Step 2:
8 (the ones digit of 18) is greater than 6 (the ones digit of 46) so Farkan regroups 1 tens block as 10 ones blocks.

tens	ones
3	16

Step 3:
Farkan subtracts 18 (he takes away 1 tens block and 8 ones blocks).

tens	ones
2	8

Here is how Farkan uses numerals to show his work:

$$46 - 18$$

Here is how Farkan shows the regrouping:

$$\begin{array}{r} ^{3}\,^{16}\\ \cancel{46}\\ -\,18 \end{array}$$

And now Farkan can subtract 16 − 8 ones and 3 − 1 tens:

$$\begin{array}{r} ^{3}\,^{16}\\ \cancel{46}\\ -\,18\\ \hline 28 \end{array}$$

---

1. In these questions, Farkan doesn't have enough ones to subtract. Help him by regrouping 1 tens block as 10 ones. Show how he would rewrite his subtraction statement.

a) 63 − 26

tens	ones
6	3

	6	3
−	2	6

tens	ones
5	13

	5	13
	6	3
−	2	6

b) 64 − 39

tens	ones
6	4

	6	4
−	3	9

tens	ones

	6	4
−	3	9

c) 42 − 19

tens	ones
4	2

	4	2
−	1	9

tens	ones

	4	2
−	1	9

d) 35 − 27

tens	ones
3	5

	3	5
−	2	7

tens	ones

	3	5
−	2	7

jump math
MULTIPLYING POTENTIAL.

Number Sense 1

2. Subtract by regrouping. The first one is done for you.

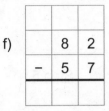

a)

	3	13
	4̸	3̸
−	2	7
	1	6

b)

	5	6
−	1	8

c)

	6	4
−	3	9

d)

	7	6
−	2	8

e)

	5	5
−	3	7

f)

	8	2
−	5	7

g)

	3	8
−	1	9

h)

	2	2
−		6

i)

	4	4
−		9

j)

	9	3
−	7	5

3. For the questions where you need to regroup, write "Help!" in the space provided. If you don't need to regroup, write "OK". Then find the answer.

a)
```
  4 14
  5̸4̸
- 19
  3 5
```
Help!
4 is less than 9

b)
```
  77
- 56
  21
```
OK

c)
```
  85
- 53
```
_____

d)
```
  95
- 18
```
_____

e)
```
  66
- 54
```
_____

f)
```
  84
- 17
```
_____

g)
```
  82
- 29
```
_____

h)
```
  26
- 15
```
_____

i)
```
  15
-  9
```
_____

j)
```
  12
-  8
```
_____

k)
```
  36
- 19
```
_____

l)
```
  52
-  9
```
_____

m)
```
  47
- 19
```
_____

n)
```
  23
-  8
```
_____

o)
```
  60
- 49
```
_____

p)
```
  82
- 41
```
_____

q)
```
  93
- 24
```
_____

r)
```
  79
- 42
```
_____

4. Subtract by regrouping the hundreds as tens. The first one has been started for you.

a)
	2	11	
	~~3~~	~~4~~	5
−	1	6	2

b)
	5	3	8
−	2	9	5

c)
	3	1	7
−	1	8	6

d)
	9	4	2
−	5	7	0

5. For the questions below, you will have to regroup <u>twice</u>.

> *Example:* Step 1 Step 2 Step 3 Step 4 Step 5
>
> Step 1:
> ```
>     4 14
> 8 5 4
> - 3 6 7
> ```
>
> Step 2:
> ```
>     4 14
> 8 5 4
> - 3 6 7
>       7
> ```
>
> Step 3:
> ```
>   7 4 14
> 8 5 4
> - 3 6 7
>       7
> ```
>
> Step 4:
> ```
>   7 4 14
> 8 5 4
> - 3 6 7
>     8 7
> ```
>
> Step 5:
> ```
>   7 4 14
> 8 5 4
> - 3 6 7
>   4 8 7
> ```

a)
	6	3	4
−	1	5	6

b)
	5	8	5
−		9	6

c)
	5	0	2
−	2	3	5

d)
	8	5	4
−	3	7	7

6. To subtract 3 245 − 1 923, Sara regroups 1 thousands block as 10 hundreds blocks.

thousands	hundreds	tens	ones	thousands	hundreds	tens	ones	thousands	hundreds	tens	ones
3	2	4	5	2	12	4	5	2	3	2	2

 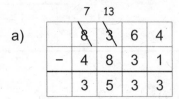 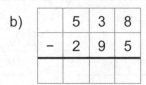 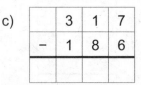

Subtract by regrouping 1 thousand as 10 hundreds. The first one has been done for you.

a)
	7	13		
	~~8~~	~~3~~	6	4
−	4	8	3	1
	3	5	3	3

b)
	5	6	9	3
−	2	7	1	1

c)
	5	7	5	8
−	2	9	4	2

7. Regroup where necessary.

a)
	3	3	1	7
−	1	4	0	5

b)
	6	4	6	8
−	2	1	7	2

c)
	7	2	6	5
−	3	0	4	2

8. In the questions below, you will have to regroup two or <u>three times.</u>

a)
	8	5	3	2
−	2	7	5	4

b)
	7	6	4	1
−	4	7	5	3

c)
	6	1	3	0
−	2	2	8	3

d)
	4	3	0	2
−	1	7	2	3

e)
	3	8	5	1
−	1	9	0	9

f)
	2	8	2	3
−	1	3	2	9

g)
	5	2	8	6
−	1	7	9	8

h)
	9	2	5	7
−	4	5	2	8

9. In the questions below you will have to regroup two or three times

Example:

 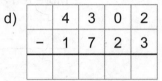

Step 1	Step 2	Step 3	Step 4

a)
	1	0	0	0
−		4	5	7

b)
	1	0	0
−		7	5

c)
	1	0	0	0
−		6	3	3

d)
	1	0	0	0
−		8	8	9

10. Subtract in your notebook, regrouping where necessary.

a) 8 504 − 1 230   b) 4 484 − 2 511   c) 4 302 − 1 723   d) 1 000 − 769

TEACHER:
See the Teacher's Guide for a fast method of performing subtractions when the number you are subtracting from is 100, 1000, 10000 and so on. (for instance, 1 000 − 723).

NS4-21: Parts and Totals

1. The bars in each picture repressent a quantity of red and green apples. Fill in the blanks.

   a) 5 red apples
       3 green apples

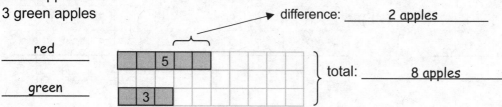

difference: ___2 apples___

total: ___8 apples___

   b) 4 green apples
       2 more red apples than green apples

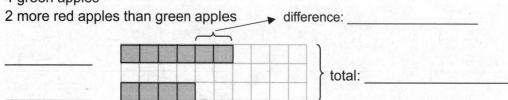

difference: _____

total: _____

   c) 7 green apples
       3 more green apples than red apples

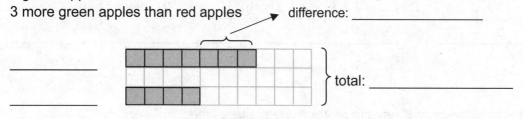

difference: _____

total: _____

   d) 10 apples in total
       3 green apples

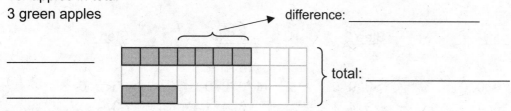

difference: _____

total: _____

2. Write the missing numbers.

Red Apples	Green Apples	Total Number of Apples	How many more of one colour of apple?
2	5	7	3 more green apples than red
3		8	
	2	9	
4			1 more red apple than green

3. Draw a picture (as in Question 1) and make a chart for each question.

   a) 4 red apples
       4 more green apples
       than red apples

   b) 12 apples in total
       7 green apples

   BONUS
   c) 10 apples in total
       2 more red apples than
       green apples

NS4-22: Parts and Totals (Advanced)

1. The fact family for the addition statement **2 + 4 = 6** is: **4 + 2 = 6**; **6 − 4 = 2** and **6 − 2 = 4**.
   Write the fact family of equations for the following statements.

   a) 3 + 4 = 7 _____

   b) 5 + 4 = 9 _____

2. Fill in the chart.

	Green Grapes	Purple Grapes	Total Number of Grapes	Fact Family		How many more of one type of grape?
a)	7	2	9	9 − 2 = 7 9 − 7 = 2	7 + 2 = 9 2 + 7 = 9	5 more green than purple
b)	6		10			
c)	2	9				
d)		5				4 more green than purple

3. Use the correct symbol (+ or −).

   a) number of red apples ☐ number of green apples = total number of apples

   b) number of red apples ☐ number of green apples = how many more red than green?

   c) number of green grapes ☐ number of purple grapes = how many more green than purple?

   d) number of purple grapes ☐ number of green grapes = total number of grapes

4. Draw a picture on grid paper (as in Question 1 on the previous page) for each question.

   a) Ron has 13 red stickers and 6 blue stickers.
      How many stickers does he have?

   b) Claire has 6 pets, 2 are dogs.
      The rest are cats. How many cats does she have?

   c) Peter walked 7 km. Layi walked 3 km.
      How much further did Peter walk?

Answer the following questions in your notebook.

1. A glass can hold 255 mL of water.
   How much water can 2 glasses hold?

2. Alice's class raised $312 for charity. Sophie's class raised $287.

   a) Whose class raised more money? How do you know?

   b) How much money did the two classes raise altogether?

3. At a summer camp, 324 children are enrolled in baseball. There are 128 <u>more</u> children enrolled in swimming than in baseball.

   a) How many children are enrolled in swimming?

   b) How many children are enrolled in lessons altogether?

4. What is the greatest number you can add to 275 without having to regroup any place value?

   # 275

5. Emma flies 2 457 km on one day and 1 357 km the next day.
   How many kilometres did she fly in the two days?

6. The world's tallest tree is 110 m tall. The Skylon Tower in Niagara Falls is 156 m tall.
   How much taller is the Skylon Tower than the tallest tree?

7. 2 375 people attended a science fair one day, and 3 528 people attended the next day.
   How many people attended the fair on both days?

8. The length of Whistling Cave on Vancouver Island is 780 m. The length of Grueling Cave is 700 m.
   How much longer is Whistling Cave than Grueling Cave?

9. The border between the United States and Canada is about 8 960 km long.
   The total length of the Great Wall of China, including its branches, is 6 320 km.
   How much longer than the Great Wall of China is the Canadian / US border?

NS4-24: Larger Numbers (Advanced)

1. Beside each number, write the place value of the underlined digit.

a) 1 2 6 4 3

> thousands

b) 2 3 1 2 1

c) 6 0 1 7 2

d) 9 3 7 5

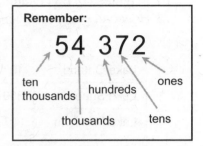

Remember:

54 372

ten thousands
hundreds
ones
thousands
tens

2. Write a numeral for the following number words:

a) twenty-two thousand, five hundred forty-four

b) one thousand, four hundred twenty

c) sixty-three thousand, nine hundred thirty-six

d) ninety-nine thousand, nine hundred one

3. Write the number words for the following numerals:

a) 61 145 = _____

b) 84 929 = _____

4. Write the number in expanded form (using numerals).

a) 17359 = _10 000 + 7000 + 300 + 50 + 9_

b) 14 972 = _____

c) 72 664 = _____

d) 92 425 = _____

e) 50 137 = _____

f) 20 001 = _____

5. Circle the greater number.

a) 14 727 or 25 848

b) 32 165 or 32 166

c) 98 400 or 97 500

6. Add or subtract.

a)
```
    1 4 2 6 3
  + 7 2 3 3 4
  _____
```

b)
```
    7 7 6 5 1
  + 1 2 3 4 8
  _____
```

c)
```
    8 1 6 4 2
  +     9 3 2 1
  _____
```

d)
```
    7 2 3 4 7
  - 3 1 1 1 2
  _____
```

e)
```
    5 7 8 3 6
  - 1 7 4 1 2
  _____
```

f)
```
    1 0 0 0 0
  -     7 1 6 2
  _____
```

Answer the following questions in your notebook.

1. In a class of 62 children, 17 are boys. How many girls are in the class? Show your work.
    How can you check your answer using addition?

2.

Lake Ontario	193 km
Lake Superior	350 km
Lake Michigan	307 km
Lake Huron	206 km
Lake Erie	241 km

This chart shows the lengths of the Great Lakes.

a) Write the lengths in order from shortest to longest.

b) How much longer than Lake Huron is Lake Michigan?

c) How much longer than the shortest lake is the longest lake?

3. Use the numbers 1, 2, 3, 4, 5, 6 to make the greatest
    sum possible and the greatest difference.

 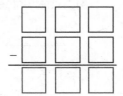

4. Find the error in Ezra's sum.

$$\begin{array}{r} 2 \\ 4\,5 \\ +\ 2\,7 \\ \hline 8\,1 \end{array}$$

5. Leonardo da Vinci, the great Italian inventor and artist, lived from 1452 to 1519.

    a) How old was he when he died?

    b) Leonardo painted his masterpiece the Mona Lisa in 1503. How old was he then?

6. Write the number that is ...
    a) ten less than 1000   b) ten more than 1000

    c) 100 less than 1000   d) 100 more than 1000

7. Pens cost 49¢. Erasers cost 45¢. Ben has 95¢. Does he have enough money to buy
    a pen and an eraser? (Explain your answer.)

8. Josh wants to add the numbers below. He starts by adding the ones digits.

    Explain why Josh wrote
    the number 1 here. ⟶
    $$\begin{array}{r} 1 \\ 3\,5 \\ +\ 4\,7 \\ \hline 2 \end{array}$$

NS4-26: Arrays

When you multiply a pair of numbers, the result is called the **product** of the numbers.

row

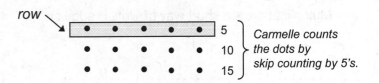

Carmelle counts the dots by skip counting by 5's.

In the **array** shown, there are 3 **rows** of dots.
There are 5 dots **in each row**.

Carmelle writes a multiplication statement for the array: **3 × 5 = 15**   (3 rows of 5 dots is 15 dots)

----

1. How many rows? How many dots in each row? Write a multiplication statement for each array.

a)

b)

c)

___3___ rows

___4___ dots in each row

___3 × 4 = 12_____

_____ rows

_____ dots in each row

_____

_____

_____

_____

2. Write a product for each array.

a)

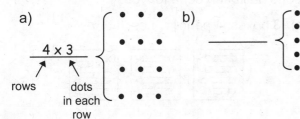

___4 × 3___

rows   dots in each row

b)

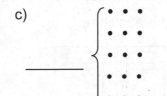

c)

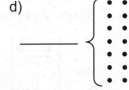

d)

3. Draw arrays for these products.

a) 5 × 5

b) 3 × 5

c) 2 × 4

d) 4 × 3

e) 1 × 6

f) 0 × 5

4. Draw an array and write a multiplication statement to find each answer.

a) In a garden, there are 3 rows of plants. There are 5 plants in each row. How many plants are there altogether?

b) On a bus, 4 people can sit in a row. There are 6 rows of seats on the bus. How many people can ride on the bus?

c) Jenny planted 8 seeds in each row. There are 4 rows of seeds. How many seeds did Jenny plant?

5. Draw arrays for the products 4 × 3 and 3 × 4.

a) Are the products the same or different?

b) Is 6 × 4 equal to 4 × 6? Explain.

NS4-27: Multiplication and Addition

Multiplication is a short way of writing addition:

$4 \times 5 = 5 + 5 + 5 + 5$

add 5 four times

----

1. Write a sum for each product. The first one has been done for you.

   a) $3 \times 4 = 4 + 4 + 4$ b) $2 \times 8 =$ c) $5 \times 6 =$

   d) $4 \times 2 =$ e) $3 \times 5 =$ f) $6 \times 3 =$

   g) $5 \times 7 =$ h) $2 \times 1 =$ i) $1 \times 8 =$

2. Write a product for each sum. The first one is done for you.

   a) $4 + 4 + 4 = 3 \times 4$ b) $5 + 5 + 5 =$ c) $4 + 4 =$

   d) $7 + 7 + 7 + 7 =$ e) $9 + 9 =$ f) $8 + 8 + 8 =$

   g) $2 + 2 + 2 =$ h) $9 + 9 + 9 + 9 =$ i) $1 + 1 + 1 =$

   j) $6 + 6 + 6 + 6 + 6 =$ k) $8 + 8 + 8 + 8 + 8 + 8 =$ l) $3 + 3 + 3 + 3 =$

3. Write a sum and a product for each picture. The first one has been done for you.

   a) 3 boxes; 2 pencils in each box

   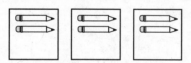

   $2 + 2 + 2$

   3×2

   b) 3 boxes; 4 pencils in each box

   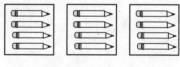

   _____

   _____

   c) 4 boxes; 3 pencils in each box

   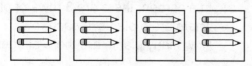

   _____

   _____

   d) 2 boxes; 5 pencils in each box

   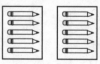

   _____

   _____

   e) 5 boxes; 3 pencils in each box

   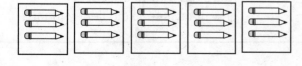

   _____

   _____

   f) 4 boxes; 2 pencils in each box

   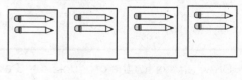

   _____

   _____

NS4-27: Multiplication and Addition (continued)

4. Add the numbers. Write your subtotals in the boxes provided.

Example   4 + 5 + 7 = ___   →add 4 + 5 (= 9)   ⬚ 9   4 + 5 + 7 = ___   →add 9 + 7 (= 16)   ⬚ 9   4 + 5 + 7 = 16

⬚ a) 2 + 3 + 5 = ___   ⬚ b) 3 + 3 + 7 = ___   ⬚ c) 5 + 4 + 3 = ___

⬚ d) 6 + 4 + 2 = ___   ⬚ e) 8 + 3 + 4 = ___   ⬚ f) 9 + 1 + 6 = ___

⬚⬚ g) 4 + 3 + 3 + 2 = ___   ⬚⬚ h) 4 + 5 + 5 + 3 = ___   ⬚⬚ i) 6 + 7 + 3 + 5 = ___

5. Write a sum for each picture. Add to find out how many apples there are altogether. Check your answer by counting the apples.

a) 3 boxes; 3 apples in each box

_____

b) 4 boxes; 2 apple in each box

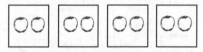

_____

c) 4 boxes; 4 apples in each box

_____

d) 3 boxes; 5 apples in each box

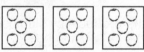

_____

6. Draw a picture and write an addition statement and a multiplication statement for your picture.

   a) 3 vans
      7 people in each van

   b) 4 bags
      5 books in each bag

   c) 6 boxes
      4 pens in each box

   d) 5 boats
      4 kids in each boat

7. Write an addition statement and a multiplication statement for each question.

   a) 6 plates
      8 cookies in each plate

   b) 7 packets
      3 gifts in each packet

   c) 4 baskets
      7 bananas in each basket

Zainab finds the product of **3** and **5** by skip counting on a number line.

She counts off three 5s.   **3 × 5 =**   **5** + **5** + **5** = **15**

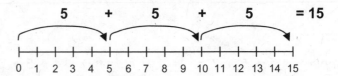

0 1 2 3 4 5 6 7 8 9 10 11 12 13 14 15

From the picture, Zainab can see that the **product** of 3 and 5 is 15.

---

1. Show how to find the products by skip counting. Use arrows like the ones in Zainab's picture.

   a) **4 x 3 =**   b) **7 x 2 =**

0 1 2 3 4 5 6 7 8 9 10 11 12 13 14 15

0 1 2 3 4 5 6 7 8 9 10 11 12 13 14 15

2. Use the number line to skip count by 4s, 6s and 7s. Fill in the boxes as you count.

0 1 2 3 4 5 6 7 8 9 **10** 11 12 13 14 15 16 17 18 19 **20** 21 22 23 24 25 26 27 28 29 **30** 31 32 33 34 35 36 37 38 39 **40** 41 42

a)   b)   c)

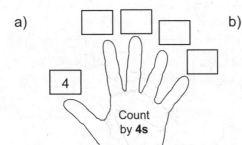
4
Count by **4s**

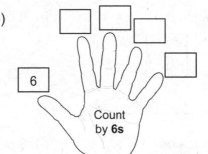
6
Count by **6s**

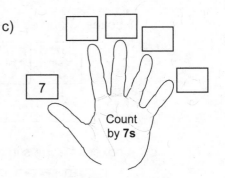
7
Count by **7s**

3. Find the products by skip counting on your fingers. Use the hands from Question 2 to help.

   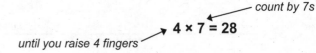

7   14   21   28

count by 7s
until you raise 4 fingers   **4 × 7 = 28**

   a) 4 × 5 =   b) 5 × 2 =   c) 4 × 4 =   d) 2 x 6 =   e) 7 × 1 =
   f) 3 × 7 =   g) 3 × 3 =   h) 6 × 1 =   i) 2 × 7 =   j) 5 × 5 =
   k) 2 × 2 =   l) 3 × 7 =   m) 2 × 1 =   n) 4 × 6 =   o) 3 × 6 =

4. Find the number of items by skip counting. Write a multiplication statement for each picture.

   a)   b)

Number Sense 1

NS4-29: Multiplying by Adding On

Marisol knows how to find 3 × 6 by adding three 6s (6 + 6 + 6 = 18). Her teacher asks her how she can find 4 × 6 <u>quickly</u> (without adding four 6s).

Marisol knows that 4 × 6 is one more 6 than 3 × 6. She shows this in two ways:

<u>With a picture</u>

<u>By adding</u>

four 6s three 6s

plus one more 6

$4 × 6 = 6 + 6 + 6 + 6$

four 6s   three 6s   plus one more 6

three 6s   plus one more 6

Marisol knows that: **4 × 6 = 3 × 6 + 6**

So she finds 4 × 6 by adding 6 to 3 × 6 (= 18): 4 × 6 = **18** + 6 = **24**

----

1. Write a product for each array.

a) $4 × 3$

rows   dots
         in each
         row

b)

c)

d)

2. Fill in the missing products.

a) $4 × 5$

rows   dots in
        each row

$3 × 5$

$+ \quad 5$

b)

$+$

c)

$+$

d)

$+$

e)

$+$

f)

$+$

3. Fill in the missing products. Then write a multiplication statement.

a)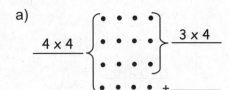

4×4 3×4

$+$ _____

_____
$4 \times 4 = 3 \times 4 + 4$

b)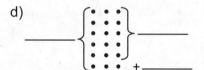

_____   _____

$+$ _____

_____

c) _____   _____

$+$ _____

_____

d) _____   _____

$+$ _____

_____

4. You can always turn a product into a smaller product and a sum.

$$5 \times 3 = \mathbf{4} \times 3 + \mathbf{3}$$

Take 1 away from 5.   *Add an extra 3.*

$$9 \times 4 = \mathbf{8} \times 4 + \mathbf{4}$$

Take 1 away from 9.   *Add an extra 4.*

Turn each product into a smaller product and a sum.

a) $4 \times 2 = 3 \times \underline{\ 2\ } + \underline{\quad}$

b) $5 \times 7 = 4 \times \underline{\quad} + \underline{\quad}$

c) $8 \times 3 = 7 \times \underline{\quad} + \underline{\quad}$

d) $3 \times 6 = 2 \times \underline{\quad} + \underline{\quad}$

e) $7 \times 4 = \underline{\quad} \times \underline{\quad} + \underline{\quad}$

f) $9 \times 6 = \underline{\quad} \times \underline{\quad} + \underline{\quad}$

g) $5 \times 3 = \underline{\hspace{4cm}}$

h) $8 \times 7 = \underline{\hspace{5cm}}$

i) $7 \times 6 = \underline{\hspace{5cm}}$

j) $6 \times 4 = \underline{\hspace{5cm}}$

5. Find each answer by turning the product into a smaller product and a sum.

a) $5 \times 3 = 4 \times 3 + 3$
   $= 12 + 3$
   $= 15$

b) $6 \times 3 =$
   $=$
   $=$

c) $6 \times 4 =$
   $=$
   $=$

d) $4 \times 4 =$
   $=$
   $=$

e) 6×6 f) 3×7 g) 7×5 h) 6×8

NS4-30: Multiples of 10

To multiply 3×20, Christie makes 3 groups containing 2 tens blocks (20 = 2 tens).

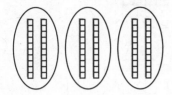

$3 \times 20 = 3 \times 2$ tens $= 6$ tens $= 60$

To multiply 3×200, Christie makes 3 groups containing 2 hundreds blocks (200 = 2 hundreds).

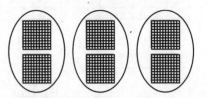

$3 \times 200 = 3 \times 2$ hundreds $= 6$ hundreds $= 600$

Christie notices a pattern: $3 \times 2 = 6$ $3 \times 20 = 60$ $3 \times 200 = 600$

----

1. Draw a model for each multiplication statement, then calculate the answer. The first one is started.

   a) 4×20

   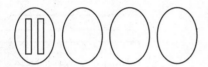

   $4 \times 20 = 4 \times$ __2__ tens = ____ tens = ____

   b) 2×30

   $2 \times 30 = 2 \times$ ____ tens = ____ tens = ____

2. Regroup to find the answer. The first one is done for you.

   a) $3 \times 70 = 3 \times$ ___7___ tens = ___21___ tens = ___210___

   b) $3 \times 50 = 3 \times$ _____ tens = _____ tens = _____

   c) $5 \times 50 = 5 \times$ _____ tens = _____ tens = _____

   d) $4 \times 60 = 4 \times$ _____ tens = _____ tens = _____

3. Complete the pattern by multiplying.

   a) $2 \times 2 =$ _____
      $2 \times 20 =$ _____
      $2 \times 200 =$ _____

   b) $5 \times 1 =$ _____
      $5 \times 10 =$ _____
      $5 \times 100 =$ _____

   c) $2 \times 4 =$ _____
      $2 \times 40 =$ _____
      $2 \times 400 =$ _____

   d) $3 \times 3 =$ _____
      $3 \times 30 =$ _____
      $3 \times 300 =$ _____

4. Multiply.

   a) $4 \times 30 =$ _____
   b) $5 \times 30 =$ _____
   c) $4 \times 40 =$ _____
   d) $2 \times 50 =$ _____

   e) $3 \times 100 =$ _____
   f) $4 \times 500 =$ _____
   g) $3 \times 60 =$ _____
   h) $6 \times 400 =$ _____

   i) $2 \times 700 =$ _____
   j) $6 \times 70 =$ _____
   k) $8 \times 40 =$ _____
   l) $2 \times 900 =$ _____

5. Draw a base ten model (using cubes to represent thousands) to show: $4 \times 1000 = 4\,000$.

6. Knowing that $3 \times 2 = 6$, how can you use this fact to multiply $3 \times 2\,000$?

jump math
MULTIPLYING POTENTIAL.

Number Sense 1

1. Write a multiplication statement for each array.

a)

3×20

b)

c)

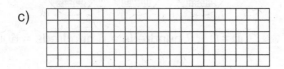

d)

2. Write a multiplication statement for the whole array and each part of the array (as shown in a).

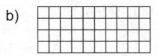

a)

3×24

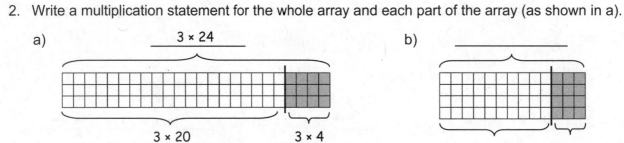

3×20 3×4

b)

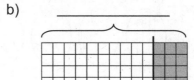

c)

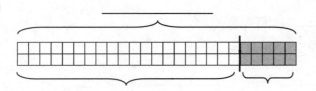

d)

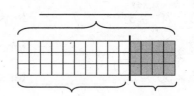

3. Fill in the blanks (as shown in a).

2×24

a)

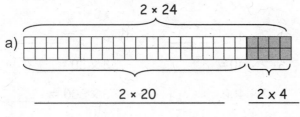

2×20 2×4

$2 \times 24 = 2 \times 20 + 2 \times 4$

b)

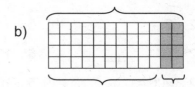

4×25

c)

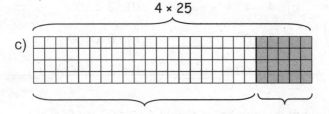

d)

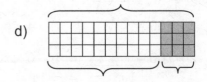

NS4-32: Mental Math

To multiply 3×23, Rosa rewrites 23 as a sum:

$$23 = 20 + 3$$

She multiplies 20 by 3: **$3 \times 20 = 60$**

Then she multiplies 3×3: **$3 \times 3 = 9$**

Finally she adds the result: **$60 + 9 = 69$**

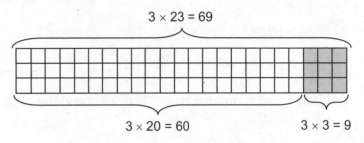

$$3 \times 23 = 69$$
$$3 \times 20 = 60 \qquad 3 \times 3 = 9$$

The picture shows why Rosa's method works: **$3 \times 23 = 3 \times 20 + 3 \times 3 = 60 + 9 = 69$**

---

1. Rewrite each multiplication statement as a sum.

   a) $2 \times 24 = \underline{\quad 2 \times 20 \quad} + \underline{\quad 2 \times 4 \quad}$

   b) $2 \times 23 = \underline{\qquad\qquad} + \underline{\qquad\qquad}$

   c) $3 \times 32 = \underline{\qquad\qquad} + \underline{\qquad\qquad}$

   d) $4 \times 12 = \underline{\qquad\qquad} + \underline{\qquad\qquad}$

2. Multiply using Rosa's method. The first one has been done for you.

   a) $3 \times 13 = \underline{\quad 3 \times 10 \quad} + \underline{\quad 3 \times 3 \quad} = \underline{\quad 30 + 9 \quad} = \underline{\quad 39 \quad}$

   b) $3 \times 21 = \underline{\qquad\qquad} + \underline{\qquad\qquad} = \underline{\qquad\qquad} = \underline{\qquad\qquad}$

   c) $2 \times 14 = \underline{\qquad\qquad} + \underline{\qquad\qquad} = \underline{\qquad\qquad} = \underline{\qquad\qquad}$

   d) $3 \times 213 = \underline{\; 3 \times 200 \;} + \underline{\; 3 \times 10 \;} + \underline{\; 3 \times 3 \;} = \underline{\; 600 + 30 + 9 \;} = \underline{\; 639 \;}$

   e) $2 \times 231 = \underline{\qquad\qquad} + \underline{\qquad\qquad} + \underline{\qquad\qquad} = \underline{\qquad\qquad} = \underline{\qquad\qquad}$

   f) $2 \times 342 = \underline{\qquad\qquad} + \underline{\qquad\qquad} + \underline{\qquad\qquad} = \underline{\qquad\qquad} = \underline{\qquad\qquad}$

3. Multiply in your head by multiplying the digits separately.

   a) $3 \times 12 = \underline{\qquad}$ b) $2 \times 31 = \underline{\qquad}$ c) $4 \times 12 = \underline{\qquad}$ d) $5 \times 11 = \underline{\qquad}$

   e) $4 \times 21 = \underline{\qquad}$ f) $2 \times 43 = \underline{\qquad}$ g) $2 \times 32 = \underline{\qquad}$ h) $3 \times 33 = \underline{\qquad}$

   i) $4 \times 112 = \underline{\qquad}$ j) $2 \times 234 = \underline{\qquad}$ k) $3 \times 233 = \underline{\qquad}$ l) $5 \times 111 = \underline{\qquad}$

   m) $3 \times 132 = \underline{\qquad}$ n) $2 \times 422 = \underline{\qquad}$ o) $4 \times 212 = \underline{\qquad}$ p) $3 \times 333 = \underline{\qquad}$

4. Yen planted 223 trees in each of 3 rows. How many trees did she plant altogether?

5. Paul put 240 marbles in each of 2 bags. How many marbles did he put in the bags?

jump math
MULTIPLYING POTENTIAL

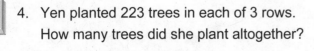

Number Sense 1

NS4-33: Mental Math: Doubling

1. Count by 2s.

    2 , 4 , 6 , _____ , _____ , _____ , _____ , _____ , _____

2. Double each number mentally by doubling the ones digit and the tens digit separately.

	24	14	12	32	64	22	13
Double	48						

	82	51	34	54	92	74	71
Double							

3. Double the ones and tens separately and add the result: $2 \times 27 = 2 \times 20 + 2 \times 7 = 40 + 14 = 54$

	16	15	25	37	28	18	48
Double							

	17	45	66	35	46	29	55
Double							

4. Use doubles to find the missing products.

If	$2 \times 7 = 14$	$3 \times 7 = 21$	$4 \times 7 = 28$	$2 \times 6 = 12$
Then	$4 \times 7 =$	$6 \times 7 =$	$8 \times 7 =$	$4 \times 6 =$

$3 \times 6 = 18$	$4 \times 6 = 24$	$2 \times 8 = 16$	$4 \times 8 = 32$
$6 \times 6 =$	$8 \times 6 =$	$4 \times 8 =$	$8 \times 8 =$

$2 \times 9 = 18$	$3 \times 9 = 27$	$4 \times 9 = 36$	$2 \times 12 = 24$
$4 \times 9 =$	$6 \times 9 =$	$8 \times 9 =$	$4 \times 12 =$

5. Calculate the total cost of 2 items mentally.

   a) 2 oranges for 42¢ each _____

   b) 2 pencils for 37¢ each _____

   c) 2 stamps for 48¢ each _____

   d) 2 gold fish for 35¢ each _____

Clara uses a chart to multiply 3 × 42:

Step 1
She multiplies the ones digit
of 42 by 3. (3 × 2 = 6)

Step 2
She multiplies the tens digit
of 42 by 3 (3 × 4 tens = 12 tens).

She regroups 10 tens
as 1 hundred.

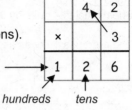

hundreds   tens

1. Use Clara's method to find the products.

a) 31 × 4

b) 53 × 2

c) 41 × 4

d) 21 × 6

e) 31 × 3

f) 71 × 2

g) 62 × 3

h) 84 × 2

i) 52 × 4

j) 22 × 2

k) 21 × 5

l) 53 × 3

m) 42 × 4

n) 43 × 3

o) 64 × 2

p) 73 × 3

q) 54 × 2

r) 62 × 4

s) 72 × 3

t) 91 × 2

u) 63 × 3

v) 81 × 2

w) 51 × 5

x) 72 × 4

y) 61 × 5

z) 72 × 2

aa) 83 × 3

bb) 91 × 9

cc) 41 × 6

dd) 61 × 8

ee) 92 × 4

ff) 85 × 1

gg) 43 × 2

hh) 61 × 7

ii) 71 × 8

2. Find the following products.

a) 3 × 62   b) 2 × 74   c) 5 × 21   d) 4 × 62   e) 5 × 41   f) 7 × 21

Jane uses a chart to multiply 3 × 24:

<u>Step 1</u>
She multiples 4 ones by 3 (4 × 3 = 12).

She regroups 10 ones as 1 ten.

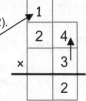

<u>Step 2</u>
She multiples 2 tens by 3 (3 × 2 tens = 6 tens).

She adds 1 ten to the result (6 + 1 = 7 tens):

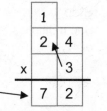

1. Using Jane's method, complete the first step of the multiplication. The first one has been done.

a)
```
  2
  1 4
×   5
─────
    0
```

b)
```
  1 4
×   3
─────
```

c)
```
  1 5
×   3
─────
```

d)
```
  3 6
×   2
─────
```

e)
```
  2 5
×   4
─────
```

2. Using Jane's method, complete the second step of the multiplication.

a)
```
  1
  2 4
×   4
─────
    6
```

b)
```
  1
  1 2
×   5
─────
    0
```

c)
```
  2
  1 4
×   5
─────
    0
```

d)
```
  2
  1 4
×   6
─────
    4
```

e)
```
  1
  2 5
×   3
─────
    5
```

f)
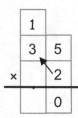
```
  1
  3 5
×   2
─────
    0
```

g)
```
  1
  4 7
×   2
─────
    4
```

h)
```
  1
  2 4
×   3
─────
    2
```

i)
```
  2
  2 7
×   3
─────
    1
```

j)
```
  3
  1 6
×   5
─────
    0
```

3. Using Jane's method, complete the first and second step of the multiplication.

a)
```
  2 5
×   2
─────
```

b)
```
  1 6
×   6
─────
```

c)
```
  3 5
×   4
─────
```

d)
```
  3 5
×   3
─────
```

> **TEACHER:**
> Be sure to give your students extra practice at this skill.

e)
```
  3 4
×   3
─────
```

f)
```
  3 2
×   5
─────
```

g)
```
  3 7
×   6
─────
```

h)
```
  8 2
×   5
─────
```

i)
```
  2 3
×   7
─────
```

NS4-36: Multiplying a 3-Digit by a 1-Digit Number

Kim multiplies 2 × 213 in 3 different ways.

1. With a chart:

hundreds	tens	ones
2	1	3
×		2
4	2	6

2. In expanded form:

$$200 + 10 + 3$$
$$\underline{\times\ 2}$$
$$= 400 + 20 + 6$$
$$= 426$$

3. With base ten materials:

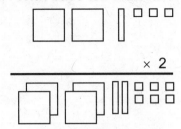

$$\times\ 2$$

---

1. Rewrite the multiplication statement in expanded notation. Then perform the multiplication.

   a) 321   _____ + _____ + _____
       × 3   _____   × 3
             = _____ + _____ + _____

             = _____

   b) 432   _____ + _____ + _____
       × 2   _____   × 2
             = _____ + _____ + _____

             = _____

2. Multiply.

   a)
   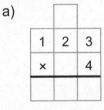
   b)
   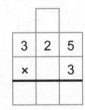
   c)
   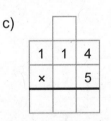
   d)
   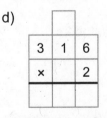
   e)
   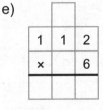

1	2	4
×		2

2	1	3
×		3

1	2	2
×		4

3	2	3
×		3

4	1	3
×		2

3. Multiply by regrouping ones as tens.

   a)

   b)
   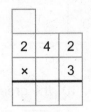
   c)
   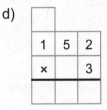
   d)
   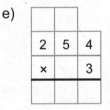
   e)

1	2	3
×		4

3	2	5
×		3

1	1	4
×		5

3	1	6
×		2

1	1	2
×		6

4. Multiply by regrouping tens as hundreds. In the last question, you will also regroup ones as tens.

   a)

2	5	2
×		4

   b)

1	5	1
×		5

   c)

2	4	2
×		3

   d)

1	5	2
×		3

   e)

2	5	4
×		3

5. Multiply.

   a) 4 × 242   b) 5 × 312   c) 7 × 123   d) 8 × 314   e) 9 × 253   f) 6 × 241

6. Draw a picture to show the result of the multiplication.

   a)
   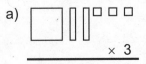
   × 3

   b)
   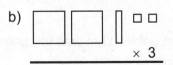
   × 3

   c)
   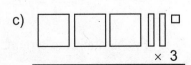
   × 3

Number Sense 1

1. Fill in the blanks.

a)

$3 \times \underline{2} + 3 \times \underline{1}$

$= 3 \times (\underline{2 + 1})$

$= 3 \times \underline{3}$

b)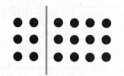

$3 \times \underline{} + 3 \times \underline{}$

$= 3 \times (\underline{} + \underline{})$

$= 3 \times \underline{}$

c)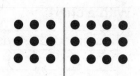

$3 \times \underline{} + 3 \times \underline{}$

$= 3 \times (\underline{} + \underline{})$

$= 3 \times \underline{}$

d) $3 \times 5 + 3 \times 4$

$= 3 \times (\underline{5 + 4})$

$= 3 \times \underline{9}$

e) $3 \times 2 + 3 \times 6$

$= 3 \times (\underline{ + })$

$= 3 \times \underline{}$

f) $7 \times 4 + 7 \times 3$

$= 7 \times (\underline{ + })$

$= 7 \times \underline{}$

2. a) Kyle: Rema:

Rema has ____ times as many stickers as Kyle.

b) Sam: Ravi:

Ravi has ____ times as many stickers as Sam.

3. Find the missing numbers.

a)

	5
x	4
1 4	

b)

	4
x	3
1 0	

c)

	7
x	5
4 3	

d)

	4
x	6
5 0	

4. Fill in the numbers 3, 4, 5 to make …   a)   the greatest product: b)   the least product:

☐ ☐ × ☐   ☐ ☐ × ☐

5. Find.

a) $0 \times 5 = \underline{}$ b) $0 \times 7 = \underline{}$ c) $0 \times 9 = \underline{}$ d) $17 \times 0 = \underline{}$

6. Eschi multiplied a number by 5 and got 0. What was the original number?

Show your work for these questions in your notebook.

1. An octopus has 240 suckers on each arm. How many suckers does an octopus have?

2. A glass holds 176 millilitres of water. How many millilitres are needed to fill 6 glasses?

3. On average, every North American uses 240 litres of water each day.

   a) About how much water does each North American use in a week?

   b) About how much water would a family of 4 use in a day?

4. The **product** of 3 and 2 is 6 (3 × 2 = 6).

   The **sum** of 3 and 2 is 5 (3 + 2 = 5).

   Which is greater: the **sum** or the **product**?

5. Try finding the **sum** and the **product** of different pairs of numbers.

   (For instance, try 3 and 4, 2 and 5, 5 and 6, 1 and 7.)

   What do you notice? Is the product always greater than the sum?

6. Kyle multiplied two numbers. The product was one of the numbers. What was the other number?

7. Write all the pairs of numbers you can think of that multiply to give 20.
   (For an extra challenge, find all pairs of numbers that multiply to give 40.)

8. An insect called a cicada can burrow into the ground and stay there for 10 years.

   a) How many months can a cicada stay in the ground?

   b) Cicadas have been known to stay in the ground for 20 years. How can you use your answer in a) to find out how many months this is?

9. There are 4 ways to put 6 dots into rows so that each row contains the same number of dots.

   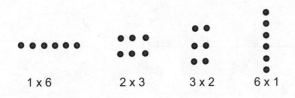

   1 x 6   2 x 3   3 x 2   6 x 1

   How many ways can you put the following number of dots into equal rows?

   Write a multiplication statement for each array.

   a) 4 dots?
   b) 8 dots?
   c) 12 dots?
   d) 16 dots?

10. Roger rode a horse around a six-sided field with each side 325 m long.

    How far did he ride?

1. Draw an arrow to the 0 or 10 to show whether the circled number is closer to **0 or 10**.

a)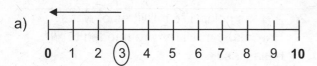

b)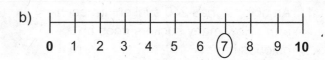

c)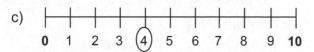

d)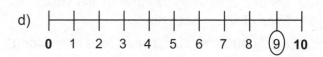

2. a) Which one digit numbers are closer to 0? _____

   b) Which are closer to 10? _____

   c) Why is 5 a special case? _____

3. Draw an arrow to show if you would round to **10 or 20 or 30**.

a)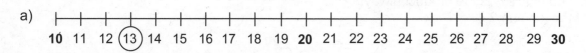

b)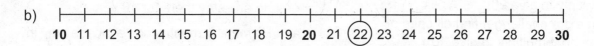

c)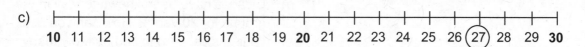

4. Draw an arrow to show which multiple of ten the number in the circle is closest to.

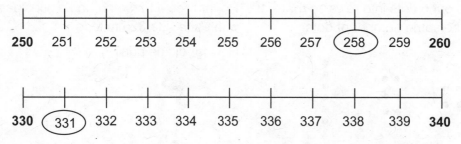

5. Circle the correct answer. Use the number lines in Questions 3 and 4 to help.

   a) 27 is closer to: 20 or 30   b) 24 is closer to: 20 or 30

   c) 19 is closer to: 10 or 20   d) 19 is closer to: 10 or 20

   e) 27 is closer to: 20 or 30   f) 12 is closer to: 10 or 20

   g) 251 is closer to: 250 or 260   h) 258 is closer to: 250 or 260

   i) 333 is closer to: 330 or 340   j) The number 339 is closer to: 330 or 340

6. Draw an arrow to show which multiple of ten you would round to. Then round each number to the nearest ten.

a)

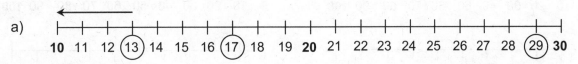

Round to: _____10_____   _____   _____

b)

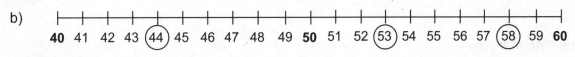

Round to: _____   _____   _____

c)

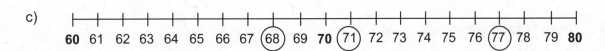

Round to: _____   _____   _____

d)

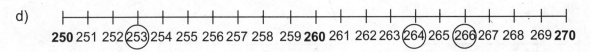

Round to: _____   _____   _____

e)

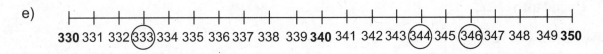

Round to: _____   _____   _____

7. Circle the correct answer. Then round the number to the nearest tens.

a) 27 is closer to 20 or 30.   Round to __30__ .

b) 16 is closer to 10 or 20.   Round to _____ .

c) 39 is closer to 30 or 40.   Round to _____ .

d) 31 is closer to 30 or 40. Round to _____ .

e) 62 is closer to 60 or 70.   Round to _____ .

f) 251 is closer to 250 or 260. Round to _____ .

g) 348 is closer to 340 or 350.   Round to _____ .

h) 258 is closer to 250 or 260. Round to _____ .

i) 341 is closer to 340 or 35.   Round to _____ .

j) 256 is closer to 250 or 260. Round to _____ .

1. Draw an arrow to show whether the circled number is closer to 0 or 100.

   a)

   0 10 20 30 40 50 60 (70) 80 90 **100**

   b)

   0 10 (20) 30 40 50 60 70 80 90 **100**

   c)

   0 10 20 30 (40) 50 60 70 80 90 **100**

   d)

   0 10 20 30 40 50 60 70 (80) 90 **100**

2. Is 50 closer to 0 or to 100? Why is 50 a special case?

   _____

3. Circle the correct answer.

   a) 80 is closer to: 0 or 100

   b) 20 is closer to: 0 or 100

   c) 40 is closer to: 0 or 100

   d) 10 is closer to: 0 or 100

   e) 60 is closer to: 0 or 100

   f) 90 is closer to: 0 or 100

4. Draw an arrow to show which multiple of 100 you would round to.

   a)
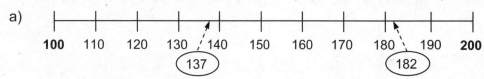

   100 110 120 130 140 150 160 170 180 190 **200**

   (137)   (182)

   Round to: _____   _____

   b)
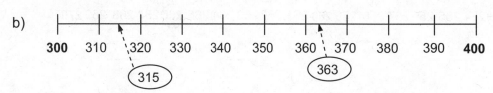

   300 310 320 330 340 350 360 370 380 390 **400**

   (315)   (363)

   Round to: _____   _____

5. Circle the correct answer.

   a) 153 is closer to: 100 or 200

   b) 189 is closer to: 100 or 200

   c) 117 is closer to: 100 or 200

   d) 135 is closer to: 100 or 200

   e) 370 is closer to: 300 or 400

   f) 332 is closer to: 300 or 400

BONUS

6. Show the approximate position of each number on the line. What multiple of 100 would you round to.

   a) 518   b) 576   c) 687   d) 629

   500 510 520 530 540 550 560 570 580 590 **600** 610 620 630 640 650 660 670 680 690 **700**

   (518)

   Round to: _____

NS4-41: Rounding a Number Line (Thousands)

1. Draw an arrow to show whether the circled number is closer to 0 or 1000.

   a)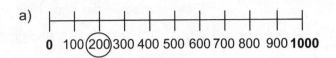

   b)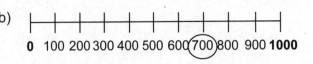

   c)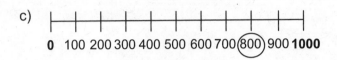

   d)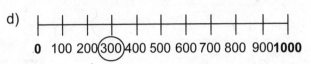

2. Is 500 closer to 0 or 1000? Why is 500 a special case?

   _____

3. Circle the correct answer.

   a) 100 is closer to 0 or 1000   b) 900 is closer to 0 or 1000

   c) 600 is closer to 0 or 1000   d) 400 is closer to 0 or 1000

4. Draw an arrow to show which multiple of 1000 you would round to.

   a)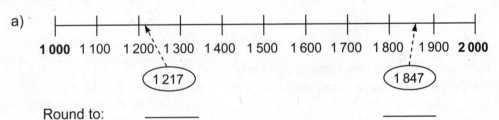

   Round to: _____   _____

   b)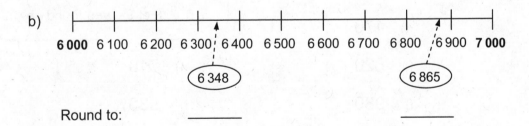

   Round to: _____   _____

5. Circle the correct answer.

   a) The number 1953 is closer to: 1000 or 2000   b) The number 6293 is closer to: 6000 or 7000

   c) The number 5521 is closer to: 5000 or 6000   d) The number 3190 is closer to: 3000 or 4000

6. Write a rule for rounding a 4-digit number to the nearest thousands.

NS4-42: Rounding

1. Round to the nearest <u>tens</u> place.

   a) 16 [ ]   b) 23 [ ]

   c) 72 [ ]   d) 66 [ ]

   e) 81 [ ]   f) 93 [ ]

   g) 14 [ ]   h) 59 [ ]

   i) 68 [ ]   j) 37 [ ]   k) 45 [ ]

   > **REMEMBER:**
   >
   > If the number in the ones digit is:
   >
   > 0, 1, 2, 3 or 4 – you round <u>down</u>
   >
   > 5, 6, 7, 8 or 9 – you round <u>up</u>

2. Round to the nearest <u>tens</u> place. Underline the tens digit first. Then put your pencil on the digit to the right (the ones digit). This digit tells you whether to round up or down.

   a) 14̲5 [150]   b) 172 [ ]   c) 320 [ ]

   d) 255 [ ]   e) 784 [ ]   f) 667 [ ]

   g) 441 [ ]   h) 939 [ ]   i) 316 [ ]

   j) 520 [ ]   k) 985 [ ]   l) 534 [ ]

   m) 758 [ ]   n) 845 [ ]   o) 293 [ ]

3. Round the following numbers to the nearest <u>hundreds</u> place. Underline the hundreds digit first. Then put your pencil on the digit to the right (the tens digit).

   > **REMEMBER:** 3̲45
   > To round to the nearest hundreds, look at the tens digit.
   >
   > 0, 1, 2, 3 or 4 – you round <u>down</u>
   >
   > 5, 6, 7, 8 or 9 – you round <u>up</u>

   a) 3̲40 [300]   b) 880 [ ]

   c) 650 [ ]   d) 170 [ ]

   e) 240 [ ]   f) 620 [ ]   g) 710 [ ]

   h) 580 [ ]   i) 980 [ ]   j) 930 [ ]

   k) 650 [ ]   l) 290 [ ]   m) 851 [ ]

   n) 158 [ ]   o) 338 [ ]   p) 411 [ ]

   q) 658 [ ]   r) 149 [ ]   s) 291 [ ]

   t) 372 [ ]   u) 868 [ ]   v) 207 [ ]

   w) 525 [ ]   x) 459 [ ]   y) 801 [ ]

NS4-42: Rounding (continued)

4. Round the following numbers to the nearest **hundreds** place. Underline the hundreds digit first. Then put your pencil on the digit to the right (the tens digit).

REMEMBER: 2$\underline{5}$31
To round to the nearest hundreds, look at the tens digit.

    0, 1, 2, 3 or 4 – you round <u>down</u>

    5, 6, 7, 8 or 9 – you round <u>up</u>

a) 2 1̲56   2 200   b) 4 389 _____

c) 3 229 _____   d) 1 905 _____   e) 5 251 _____

f) 9 127 _____   g) 6 472 _____   h) 8 783 _____

i) 7 255 _____   j) 1 098 _____   k) 3 886 _____

l) 4 624 _____   m) 8 077 _____   n) 6 382 _____

o) 9 561 _____   p) 2 612 _____   q) 5 924 _____

BONUS
r) 2 963 _____   s) 997 _____   t) 3 982 _____

5. Round the following numbers to the nearest **thousands** place. Underline the thousands digit first. Then put your pencil on the digit to the right (the hundreds digit).

REMEMBER: $\underline{7}$826
To round to the nearest thousands, look at the hundreds digit.

    0, 1, 2, 3 or 4 – you round <u>down</u>

    5, 6, 7, 8 or 9 – you round <u>up</u>

a) 2̲ 757   3 000   b) 9 052 _____

c) 6 831 _____   d) 3 480 _____

e) 5 543 _____   f) 4 740 _____   g) 8 193 _____

h) 2 607 _____   i) 6 107 _____   j) 9 125 _____

k) 5 114 _____   l) 7 649 _____   m) 1 336 _____

n) 9 538 _____   o) 4 226 _____   p) 7 311 _____

q) 8 644 _____   r) 2 750 _____   s) 9 928 _____

NS4-43: Rounding on a Grid

1. Underline the digit you wish to round to. Then say whether you would round up or down.

a) *hundreds*

| 2 | 3 | 4 | 5 |

round up
~~round down~~

b) *hundreds*

| 6 | 5 | 6 | 3 |

round up
round down

c) *hundreds*

| 3 | 8 | 5 | 2 |

round up
round down

d) *tens*

| 2 | 1 | 3 | 5 |

round up
round down

e) *tens*

| 2 | 0 | 7 | 5 |

round up
round down

f) *thousands*

| 7 | 8 | 4 | 2 |

round up
round down

2. Complete the first two steps of rounding. Then follow the steps below.

> Round the digit underlined (up or down).
>
> • To round up add 1 to the digit.
> • To round down keep the digit the same
>
>
>
> The digits to the right of the rounded digit become zeros.
>
> The digits to the left remain the same.
>
>

a) *thousands*

| 3 | 2 | 0 | 1 |

ru
rd

b) *thousands*

| 6 | 8 | 7 | 5 |

ru
rd

c) *hundreds*

| 4 | 3 | 1 | 7 |

ru
rd

d) *hundreds*

| 8 | 6 | 8 | 1 |

ru
rd

e) *tens*

| 5 | 2 | 3 | 7 |

ru
rd

f) *tens*

| 3 | 9 | 2 | 1 |

ru
rd

g) *hundreds*

| 2 | 8 | 5 | 7 |

ru
rd

h) *tens*

| 6 | 3 | 1 | 2 |

ru
rd

i) *thousands*

| 5 | 0 | 0 | 7 |

ru
rd

3. Sometimes in rounding, you have to regroup.

> *Example:*
> Round 3995 to the nearest hundred.
>
> | 3 | 9 | 8 | 5 |
> | | 10 | | |
>
> *900 rounds to 1000.*
>
> | 3 | 9 | 8 | 5 |
> | 4 | 0 | | |
>
> *Regroup the 10 hundreds as 1 (thousand) and add it to the 3 (thousand).*
>
> | 3 | 9 | 8 | 5 |
> | 4 | 0 | 0 | 0 |
>
> *Complete the rounding.*

Round each number to the digit given (regroup if necessary).

a) 2195 *tens*

b) 3942 *hundreds*

c) 9851 *thousands*

d) 13 291 *tens*

e) 4921 *hundreds*

f) 6973 *hundreds*

g) 1239 *tens*

h) 7896 *tens*

NS4-44: Estimating Sums and Differences

1. Estimate by rounding to the nearest <u>tens</u>.

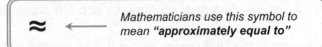

≈ ← Mathematicians use this symbol to mean **"approximately equal to"**

a) 52 → 50
    + 34 → + 30
    _____
            80

b) 19
    + 65   +
    _____

c) 47
    − 11   −
    _____

d) 95
    − 62   −
    _____

e) 32 + 11
    ≈ 30 + 10
    = 40

f) 74 + 32

g) 37 + 25

h) 84 + 28

i) 25 + 37

j) 28 − 12

k) 36 + 21

l) 85 − 17

2. Estimate by rounding to the nearest <u>hundreds</u>.

a)
    170 → 200
    + 350 → + 400
    _____
            600

b)
    190
    + 650   +
    _____

c)
    470
    − 110   −
    _____

d)
    950
    − 620   −
    _____

e) 540 + 210
    ≈

f) 550 + 330

g) 210 + 770

h) 750 + 220

i) 380 + 420

j) 871 - 543

k) 483 - 283

l) 689 + 214

3. Estimate by rounding to the nearest <u>thousands</u>.

a) 1 275 → 1000
    + 3 940 → + 4000
    _____
            5 000

b) 4 729
    − 3 132   −
    _____

c) 2 570
    + 634   +
    _____

d) 9 172
    − 4 529   −
    _____

4. Round to the nearest <u>hundreds</u>. Then find the sum or difference.

a) 3 272 + 1 235 ≈

b) 3 581 − 1 826 ≈

c) 4 821 − 3 670 ≈

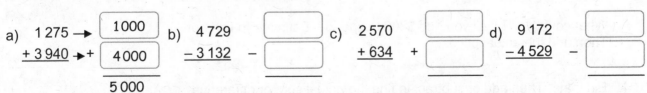

Number Sense 1

Anita collected 21 books for charity and Mark collected 28 books.

They estimated how many books they collected altogether.

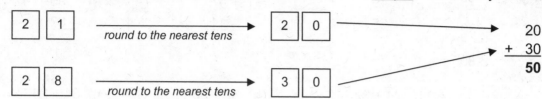

Step 1: *First they rounded the numbers to the nearest 10s.*   Step 2: *Then they added the results.*

| 2 | 1 | → round to the nearest tens → | 2 | 0 |

| 2 | 8 | → round to the nearest tens → | 3 | 0 |

```
  20
+ 30
  50
```

----

1. Estimate how many books the children collected. (Round to the nearest tens)

   a) Kishon collected 24 books and Jasjit collected 32 books.

   b) Mumtaz collected 75 books and Elizabeth collected 18 books.

   c) Annisha collected 31 books and Christina collected 56 books.

2. a) Class 4A collected 243 books and class 4B collected 456 books for charity.
      About how many books did 4A and 4B collect altogether?

   b) Class 4C collected 645 books and class 4D collected 129 books.
      About how many more books did 4C collect than 4D?

   c) About how many books did all the Grade 4s (4A, 4B, 4C, 4D) collect altogether?

----

3. A store has the following items for sale:

A. Sofa – $472   **B.** Armchair – $ 227   **C.** Table - $ 189   **D.** Desk - $382   **E.** Lamp - $ 112

What could you buy if you had $800 to spend? Estimate to find out.
Then add the actual prices.

----

4. Estimate. Then add or subtract to find the actual sum or difference.

   a) 376 + 212   b) 875 – 341   c) 907 – 588

NS4-46: More Estimating

1. Circle the products you think will be greater than 7 000. Then check your estimates.

a) 3897
   × 2

   Estimate [ ]

b) 2318
   × 3

   Estimate [ ]

c) 1387
   × 4

   Estimate [ ]

2. In **front-end estimation**, you ignore all but the first digits of the number.

$$257 + 312 \approx 200 + 300 = 500$$

Complete the chart. Does front-end estimation ever give a better result for addition?

	Round to the Nearest 100	Front-end Estimate	Actual Sum
a)	$287 + 410 \approx 300 + 400$ $= 700$	$287 + 410 \approx 200 + 400$ $= 600$	2 8 7 + 4 1 0 6 9 7
b)	$647 + 452 \approx$ $=$	$647 + 452 \approx$ $=$	6 4 7 + 4 5 2
c)	$321 + 210 \approx$	$321 + 210 \approx$ $=$	3 2 1 + 2 1 0

3. Which sums will be greater than 700? Guess and then check your guess by adding.

   a) 311 + 387   b) 452 + 286   c) 197 + 502

4. The estimated difference between two numbers is 400.
   What might the original numbers be?

5. A forest elephant weighs 4 574 kg.
   A small car weighs 1 623 kg.
   Approximately how many small cars weigh the same as an elephant?

6. Pencils are sold in boxes of 1 024.
   Approximately how many are in 8 boxes?

BONUS
7. Make up a subtraction question where front end estimating will give a better estimate than rounding to the nearest hundreds.

NS4-47: Counting Coins

1. Write the name and value of each coin.

a) Name _____ Value _____

b) Name _____ Value _____

c) Name _____ Value _____

d) Name _____ Value _____

2. Answer the following questions.

a) How many pennies do you need to make a nickel? _____

b) How many pennies do you need to make a dime? _____

c) How many nickels do you need to make a dime? _____

d) How many nickels do you need to make a quarter? _____

e) How many pennies do you need to make a quarter? _____

f) How many dimes do you need to make a quarter if you already have one nickel? _____

3. Count by 5s starting from the given numbers.

a) 80, _____, _____, _____
b) 40, _____, _____, _____
c) 60, _____, _____, _____

d) 70, _____, _____, _____
e) 105, _____, _____, _____
f) 120, _____, _____, _____

4. Count on by 5s from the given number.

a) 55, ____, ____, ____, ____
b) 75, ____, ____, ____, ____
c) 85, ____, ____, ____, ____

5. Count by 10s starting from the given numbers.

a) 30, _____, _____, _____
b) 60, _____, _____, _____
c) 80, _____, _____, _____

d) 70, _____, _____, _____
e) 100, _____, _____, _____
f) 120, _____, _____, _____

6. Count on by 10s from the given number.

a) 55, ____, ____, ____, ____
b) 70, ____, ____, ____, ____
c) 85, ____, ____, ____, ____

Number Sense 1

7. Count by the first number given, then by the second number after the vertical line.

a) __5__ , ___ , ___ , ___ , ___ | ___ , ___ , ___

   Count by 5s   *Continue counting by 1s*

b) __5__ , ___ , ___ , ___ | ___ , ___ , ___

   Count by 5s   *Continue counting by 1s*

8. Count by the first number given, then by the second number after the vertical line.

(10¢) (10¢) | (5¢) (5¢) (5¢) (5¢) (5¢)   (10¢) (10¢) (10¢) | (5¢) (5¢) (5¢) (5¢)

a) __5__ , ___ , ___ | ___ , ___ , ___ , ___ , ___

   Count by 10s   *Continue counting by 5s*

b) ___ , ___ , ___ | ___ , ___ , ___ , ___

   Count by 10s   *Continue counting by 5s*

(25¢) (25¢) (25¢) | (10¢) (10¢)   (25¢) (25¢) (25¢) | (5¢) (5¢)

c) ___ , ___ , ___ | ___ , ___

   Count by 25s   *Count by 10s*

d) ___ , ___ , ___ | ___ , ___

   Count by 25s   *Count by 5s*

9. Count by the first number given, then by the following numbers given.

a)

__25__ , __50__ , __75__ | __80__ , __85__ | __86__

Count by 25s   *Count by 5s*   *Count by 1s*

b) ___ , ___ | ___ , ___ | ___ , ___ , ___

Count by 25s   *Count by 10s*   *Count by 5s*

c) ___ , ___ | ___ | ___ , ___ , ___

Count by 25s   *Count by 10s*   *Count by 5s*

d) ___ , ___ , ___ | ___ , ___ , ___ | ___ , ___

Count by 25s   *Count by 10s*   *Count by 1s*

BONUS

e) ___ , ___ | ___ , ___ , ___ | ___ , ___ | ___ , ___

Count by 25s   *Count by 10s*   *Count by 5s*   *Count by 1s*

10. Count by the first coin value given, then by the others as the coin type changes.

(10¢) (10¢) (10¢) (5¢) (5¢) (1¢)   (5¢) (5¢) (5¢) (10¢) (10¢) (1¢)

a) __10__ , __20__ , __30__ , __35__ , __40__ , __41__

b) ___ , ___ , ___ , ___ , ___ , ___

BONUS

(25¢) (25¢) (25¢) (25¢) (10¢) (10¢) (5¢) (5¢) (5¢) (1¢) (1¢) (1¢) (1¢)

c) ___ , ___ , ___ , ___ , ___ , ___ , ___ , ___ , ___ , ___ , ___ , ___ , ___

11. Complete each pattern.

a)
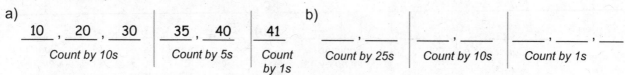

| 10 , 20 , 30 | 35 , 40 | 41 |
| Count by 10s | Count by 5s | Count by 1s |

b)
| ____ , ____ | ____ , ____ | ____ , ____ , ____ |
| Count by 25s | Count by 10s | Count by 1s |

c)
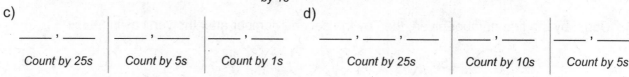

| ____ , ____ | ____ , ____ | ____ , ____ |
| Count by 25s | Count by 5s | Count by 1s |

d)
| ____ , ____ , ____ | ____ , ____ | ____ , ____ |
| Count by 25s | Count by 10s | Count by 5s |

BONUS   e)
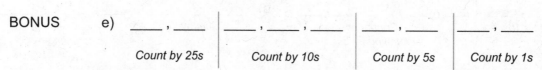

| ____ , ____ | ____ , ____ , ____ | ____ , ____ | ____ , ____ |
| Count by 25s | Count by 10s | Count by 5s | Count by 1s |

12. Write the total amount of money in cents for the number of coins given in the charts below.

   HINT: Count by the greater amount first.

a)
Nickels	Pennies
7	4

Total amount =

b)
Quarters	Dimes
4	2

Total amount =

c)
Quarters	Nickels
6	6

Total amount =

BONUS

d)
Quarters	Nickels	Pennies
3	1	2

Total amount =

e)
Quarters	Dimes	Nickels
2	2	5

Total amount =

f)
Quarters	Dimes	Nickels	Pennies
2	1	2	6

Total amount =

g)
Quarters	Dimes	Nickels	Pennies
5	3	4	9

Total amount =

13. Count the given coins and write the total amount. **HINT: Count by the greater amount first.**

a)
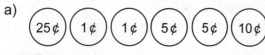

25¢ 1¢ 1¢ 5¢ 5¢ 10¢

Total amount = _____

b)

10¢ 1¢ 10¢ 25¢ 25¢ 1¢

Total amount = _____

c)

10¢ 1¢ 25¢ 5¢ 10¢ 25¢

Total amount = _____

d)

5¢ 10¢ 25¢ 5¢ 1¢ 5¢

Total amount = _____

BONUS

e)
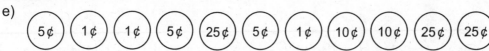

5¢ 1¢ 1¢ 5¢ 25¢ 5¢ 1¢ 10¢ 10¢ 25¢ 25¢

Total amount = _____

TEACHER: Allow your students to practise the skill in Question 13 with play money.

NS4-48: Counting by Different Denominations

1. Fill in the missing amounts, counting by 5s.

   a) 14, ____ , 24 , 29
   b) 30, ____ , ____ , 45
   c) 67, ____ , ____ , 82
   d) 18, ____ , ____ , 33
   e) 71, ____ , ____ , 86
   f) 45, ____ , ____ , 60

2. Fill in the missing amounts, counting by 10s.

   a) 63, ____ , 83
   b) 24, ____ , ____ , 54
   c) 39, ____ , ____ , 69

3. For each of the questions below, write in the missing coin to complete the addition statement. The possibilities for each question are listed.

   a) (10¢) (5¢) ( ) = 16¢   10¢ or 1¢
   b) (10¢) (5¢) ( ) = 20¢   10¢ or 5¢
   c) (10¢) (10¢) ( ) = 21¢   10¢ or 1¢
   d) (25¢) (25¢) ( ) = 75¢   25¢ or 10¢
   e) (25¢) (10¢) ( ) = 40¢   10¢ or 5¢
   f) (10¢) (5¢) ( ) = 40¢   25¢ or 5¢

4. For each question, draw in the additional <u>nickels</u> needed to make the total.

   a) (10¢) = 20¢
   b) (1¢) (1¢) = 12¢
   c) (10¢) (10¢) (1¢) = 31¢
   d) (10¢) (5¢) (1¢) = 26¢
   e) (25¢) (5¢) = 45¢
   f) (5¢) (5¢) = 40¢

5. For each question, draw in the additional <u>dimes</u> needed to make the total.

   a) (25¢) (5¢) = 50¢
   b) (25¢) (1¢) (25¢) (1¢) = 62¢
   c) (10¢) (10¢) (5¢) = 35¢
   d) (10¢) (5¢) (1¢) = 46¢
   e) (25¢) (25¢) = 80¢
   f) (5¢) (5¢) = 50¢
   g) (25¢) (25¢) (5¢) (5¢) = 80¢
   h) (25¢) (25¢) (25¢) (5¢) = 90¢
   i) (25¢) (25¢) (25¢) (5¢) = 110¢

6. For each question, draw in the additional <u>coins</u> needed to make each total.

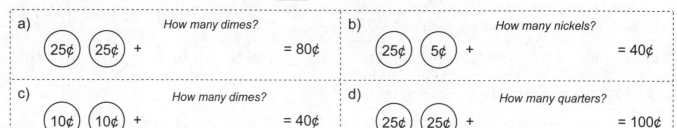

a) *How many dimes?*

(25¢)(25¢) +   = 80¢

b) *How many nickels?*

(25¢)(5¢) +   = 40¢

c) *How many dimes?*

(10¢)(10¢) +   = 40¢

d) *How many quarters?*

(25¢)(25¢) +   = 100¢

BONUS

7. Draw the additional coins needed to make each total. Use only **two** coins for each question, such as: a penny & a nickel, a penny & a dime or a nickel & a dime.

a) 21¢ (10¢)

b) 35¢ (10¢)(5¢)

c) 50¢ (25¢)(10¢)

d) 17¢ (5¢)(1¢)

e) 31¢ (10¢)(1¢)

f) 65¢ (25¢)(25¢)

8. Draw the additional coins needed to make each total. You can only use **two** coins for each question, either a loonie or a toonie.

a) $5 ($2)

b) $7 ($2)($2)

c) $3 ($1)

d) $10 ($2)($2)($2)($1)

e) $8 ($2)($2)

f) $6 ($2)($1)

9. Draw a picture to show the <u>extra</u> coins each child will need. Try to use the fewest coins.

   a) Tashi has 25¢. He wants to buy a pencil for 45¢.

   b) Zoltan has 3 quarters, a dime, and a nickel. He wants to buy a notebook for 98¢.

   c) Marzuk has 2 toonies and a loonie. He wants to buy a book for seven dollars and twenty-five cents.

10. Show how to make 80¢ using only …   a) dimes and quarters?   b) nickels and quarters?

11. Make up a problem like one of the problems in Question 9 and solve it.

1. Use the least number of coins to make the totals.
   HINT: Start by seeing how many dimes you need.

a) 12¢   (10¢)(1¢)(1¢) *correct*
          (5¢)(5¢)(1¢)(1¢) *incorrect*

b) 16¢

c) 22¢

d) 8¢

e) 15¢

f) 20¢

g) 17¢

h) 24¢

i) 11¢

j) 15¢

k) 19¢

l) 23¢

2. Fill in the amounts: a) 2 quarters = _____ ¢   b) 3 quarters = _____ ¢   c) 4 quarters = _____ ¢

3. What is the greatest amount you could pay in quarters without exceeding the amount? (Draw the quarters to show your answer.)

Amount	Greatest amount you could pay in quarters	Amount	Greatest amount you could pay in quarters
a) 35¢		b) 53¢	
c) 78¢		d) 83¢	
e) 59¢		f) 64¢	
g) 49¢		h) 31¢	
i) 82¢		j) 95¢	
k) 29¢		l) 72¢	

Number Sense 1

4. Find the greatest amount you could pay in quarters.
   Then represent the amount remaining using the least number of coins.

Amount	Amount Paid in Quarters	Amount Remaining	Amount Remaining in Coins
a) 83¢	75¢	83¢ - 75¢ = 8¢	5¢ 1¢ 1¢ 1¢
b) 56¢			
c) 33¢			
d) 85¢			
e) 97¢			

5. Use the **least** number of coins to make the totals. The first one is done for you.

   HINT: Start by finding the greatest amount you can make in quarters, as in Question 4.

a) 30¢ 10¢ 10¢ 10¢ *incorrect* 25¢ 5¢ *correct*	b) 76¢
c) 40¢	d) 53¢

6. Show how you could make 55¢ using the least number of coins. Use play money to help you.

7. Trade coins to make each amount with the least amount of coins. Draw a picture to show your final answer.

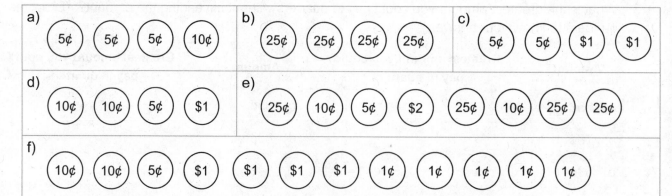

a) 5¢ 5¢ 5¢ 10¢

b) 25¢ 25¢ 25¢ 25¢

c) 5¢ 5¢ $1 $1

d) 10¢ 10¢ 5¢ $1

e) 25¢ 10¢ 5¢ $2 25¢ 10¢ 25¢ 25¢

f) 10¢ 10¢ 5¢ $1 $1 $1 $1 1¢ 1¢ 1¢ 1¢ 1¢

8. Show how you could trade the amounts for the least number of coins.

   a) 5 quarters

   b) 4 dimes and 2 nickels

   c) 6 loonies

   d) 7 loonies and 5 dimes

   e) 9 loonies, 6 dimes, 2 nickels and 5 pennies

NS4-50: Making Change Using Mental Math

1. Calculate the change owing for each purchase.

   a) Price of a pencil = 42¢
      Amount Paid = 50¢

      Change = _____

   b) Price of an eraser = 34¢
      Amount paid = 50¢

      Change = _____

   c) Price of a sharpener = 81¢
      Amount paid = 90¢

      Change = _____

   d) Price of a ruler = 56¢
      Amount Paid = 60¢

      Change = _____

   e) Price of a marker = 78¢
      Amount Paid = 80¢

      Change = _____

   f) Price of a notebook = 63¢
      Amount Paid = 70¢

      Change = _____

2. Count up by 10s to find the change owing from a dollar (100¢).

Price Paid	Change	Price Paid	Change	Price Paid	Change
a) 90¢		d) 40¢		g) 20¢	
b) 70¢		e) 10¢		h) 60¢	
c) 50¢		f) 30¢		i) 80¢	

3. Find the change owing for each purchase.
   HINT: Count up by 10s.

   a) Price of a lollipop = 50¢
      Amount Paid = $1.00

      Change = _____

   b) Price of an eraser = 60¢
      Amount paid = $1.00

      Change = _____

   c) Price of an apple = 30¢
      Amount paid = $1.00

      Change = _____

   d) Price of a banana = 60¢
      Amount Paid = $1.00

      Change = _____

   e) Price of a patty = 80¢
      Amount Paid = $1.00

      Change = _____

   f) Price of a pencil = 20¢
      Amount Paid = $1.00

      Change = _____

   g) Price of a gumball = 10¢
      Amount Paid = $1.00

      Change = _____

   h) Price of a juice = 40¢
      Amount Paid = $1.00

      Change = _____

   i) Price of a popsicle = 70¢
      Amount Paid = $1.00

      Change = _____

4. Find the smallest 2-digit number ending in zero (i.e. 10, 20, 30, 40...) that is <u>greater</u> than the number given.

   a) 72 [80]   b) 54 [ ]   c) 47 [ ]   d) 26 [ ]   e) 58 [ ]   f) 7 [ ]

 jump math
MULTIPLYING POTENTIAL.

5. Make change from $1.00 for the numbers written below. Follow the steps shown for 17¢.

Step 1:   Find the smallest multiple of 10 greater than 17¢.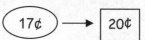

Step 2:   Find the differences.   20 – 17 *and* 100 – 20

Step 3:   Add the differences.   3¢ + 80¢   **Change = 83¢**

a)
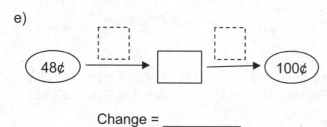

Change = _____

b)
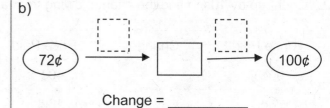

Change = _____

c)

Change = _____

d)

Change = _____

e)

Change = _____

f)
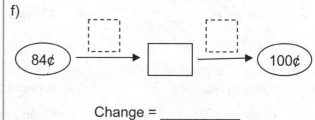

Change = _____

6. Find change from 100¢ for the following. Try to do the work in your head.

a) 58¢ _____   b) 64¢ _____   c) 27¢ _____   d) 36¢ _____   e) 52¢ _____

f) 29¢ _____   g) 97¢ _____   h) 14¢ _____   i) 89¢ _____   j) 91¢ _____

BONUS

7. Find the change for the following amount in your head.

a) Price: 37¢   Amount Paid: 50¢

b) Price: 58¢   Amount Paid: 75¢

Change Required: _____

Change Required: _____

NS4-51: Organized Lists

Many problems in mathematics and science have more than one solution.

If a problem involves two quantities, list the values of one quantity in increasing order.
Then you won't miss any solutions.

For instance, to find all the ways you can make 35¢ with dimes and nickels, start by assuming you have no dimes, then 1 dime, and so on up to 3 dimes (4 would be too many).

In each case, count on by 5s to 35 to find out how many nickels you need to make 35¢.

Step 1:

dimes	nickels
0	
1	
2	
3	

Step 2:

dimes	nickels
0	7
1	5
2	3
3	1

---

1. Fill in the amount of pennies, nickels, or dimes you need to…

a) … make 19¢

dimes	pennies
0	
1	
2	

b) … make 45¢

dimes	nickels
0	
1	
2	
3	
4	

c) … make 24¢

nickels	pennies
0	
1	
2	
3	
4	

d) … make 35¢

dimes	nickels
0	
1	
2	
3	

e) … make 80¢

quarters	nickels
0	
1	
2	
3	

f) … make 95¢

quarters	nickels
0	
1	
2	
3	

2.

quarters	nickels
0	
1	
2	

Kyle wants to find all the ways he can make 55¢ using quarters and nickels. He lists the number of quarters in increasing order. Why did he stop at 2 quarters?

_____

_____

3. Fill in the amount of pennies, nickels, dimes, or quarters you need to…

   HINT: You may not need to use all of the rows.

a) … make 13¢

dimes	pennies

b) … make 35¢

dimes	nickels

c) … make 80¢

quarters	nickels

TEACHER:

Give your students practice at questions like the one below before you allow them to continue.

4. Birds have 2 legs, cats have 4 legs, and ants have 6 legs. Complete the charts to find out how many legs each combination of 2 animals has.

a)

birds	cats	total number of legs
0	2	
1	1	
2	0	

b)

birds	ants	total number of legs
0	2	
1	1	
2	0	

5. Fill in the charts to find the solution to each problem.

a)

birds	dogs	total number of legs

Two pets have a total of 6 legs.
Each pet is either a bird or a dog.
How many birds and dogs?

b)

birds	cats	total number of legs

Three pets have a total of 8 legs.
Each pet is either a bird or cat.
How many birds and cats?

ME4-1: Estimating Lengths in Centimetres

1. A **centimetre** (cm) is a unit of measurement for **length** (or **height** or **thickness**).

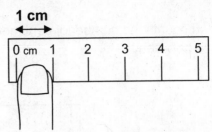

Your index finger is approximately one centimetre wide.

Measure the following objects using your index finger (or the finger that measures closest to 1 cm).

a) My pencil is approximately _____ cm long.   b) My shoe is about _____ cm long.

2. Select another object in the classroom to measure with your index finger.

_____ is approximately _____ cm.

3.

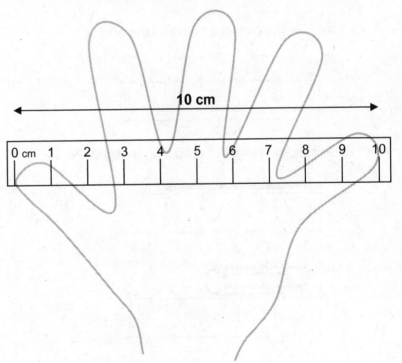

A toonie is about 3 cm wide.

How many toonies would you need to line up to make …
HINT: Skip count by 3s.

a) 15 cm? _____   b) 18 cm? _____   c) 30 cm? _____

4. Hold your hand up to a ruler.

How far do you have to spread your fingers to make your hand 10 cm wide?

Now measure the following objects using your (measured) spread-out hand.

a) My desk is approx. _____ cm long.

b) My arm is approx. _____ cm long.

5. Select more objects in the classroom to measure with your hand.

a) _____ is approximately _____cm long.

b) _____ is approximately _____cm long.

Midori counts the number of centimetres between the arrows by counting the number of "hops" it takes to move between them.

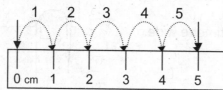

_____5_____ cm

---

1. Measure the distance between the arrows.

a) 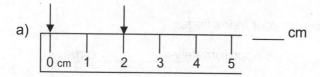 ____ cm   b) 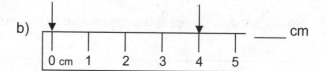 ____ cm

2. Measure the distance between the arrows. Count carefully, as the first arrow is not at the beginning of the ruler.

a) 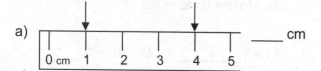 ____ cm   b) 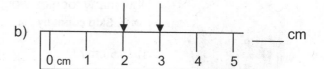 ____ cm

3. Measure the distance between the arrows.

a) 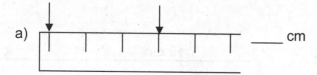 ____ cm   b) 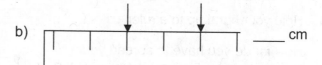 ____ cm

4. Measure the length of each line or object.

a) 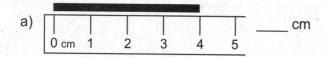 ____ cm   b) 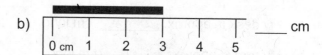 ____ cm

c) 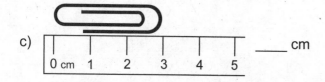 ____ cm   d) 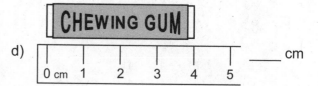 ____ cm

5. Measure the length of the line and object below.

a)  ____ cm   b) 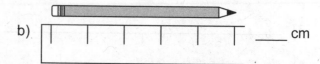 ____ cm

jump math
MULTIPLYING POTENTIAL

Measurement 1

ME4-3: Drawing and Measuring in Centimetres

1. Measure the length of each line using a ruler.

a) _____ cm

b) _____ cm

c) _____ cm

d) _____ cm

2. Measure the length of each object using a ruler.

a)

_____ cm

b)

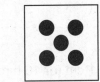

_____ cm

3. Measure all the sides of each shape.

a)

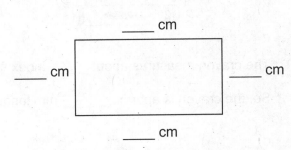

_____ cm

_____ cm

_____ cm

_____ cm

b)

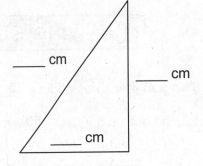

_____ cm

_____ cm

_____ cm

4. On each ruler, draw two arrows for the given distance. The first question is done for you.

a) 4 cm apart

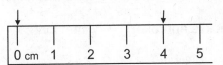

b) 3 cm apart

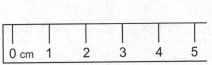

c) 5 cm apart

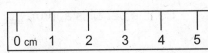

5. Using a straight edge, draw a line that is …

a) 1 cm long.

b) 4 cm long.

c) 2 cm long.

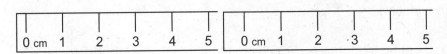

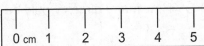

6. Draw a line …

a) 3 cm long.

b) 5 cm long.

c) 10 cm long.

7. Draw each object to the exact measurement.

a) A caterpillar – 4 cm long

b) A leaf – 11 cm long

c) A pencil – 8 cm long

8. On grid paper, draw a rectangle with a length of 5 cm and a width of 2 cm.

jump math
MULTIPLYING POTENTIAL

Measurement 1

ME4-4: Estimating in Millimetres

If you look at a ruler with millimetre measurements, you can see that 1 cm is equal to 10 mm:

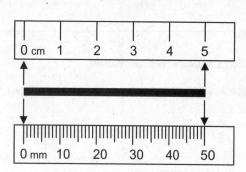

How long is the line in mm? How long is it in cm?

The line is _____ mm long, or _____ cm long.

To convert a measurement from cm to mm, we have to multiply the measurement by _____ .

---

1. Your index finger is about 1 cm (or 10 mm) wide. Measure the objects with your index finger, then convert the measurement to mm.

    a)
    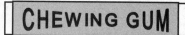

    The gum measures about ___5___ index fingers.

    So, the gum is approx. ___50___ mm long.

    b)

    The crayon measures about _____ index fingers.

    So, the crayon is approx. _____ mm long.

    c)
    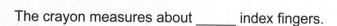

    The pencil measures about _____ index fingers.

    So, the pencil is approx. _____ mm long.

    d)

    The tack measures about _____ index fingers.

    So, the tack is approx. _____ mm long.

2. A dime is about 1 mm high. So, a stack of ten dimes would be about 1 cm high.

     1 dime = 1 mm

    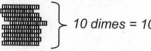 10 dimes = 10 mm = 1 cm

    How many dimes would be in a stack …

    a) 2 cm high?   b) 3 cm high?   c) 5 cm high?   d) 10 cm high?

    _____   _____   _____   _____

3. Jamelia has 4 stacks of dimes. Each stack is about 1 cm high.
    About how much money does Jamelia have? Explain.

ME4-5: Millimetres and Centimetres

Mei-Ling wants to measure a line that is 23 mm long.

Rather than counting every millimetre, Mei-Ling counts by 10s until she reaches 20. Then she counts on by ones.

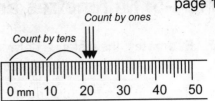

1. What is the distance between the two arrows?

a)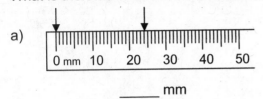

_____ mm

b)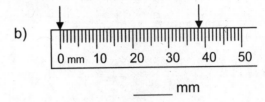

_____ mm

2. Find the length of each line.

a)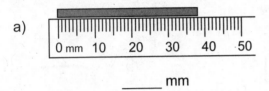

_____ mm

b)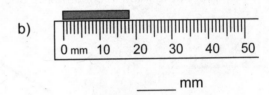

_____ mm

3. Using a straight edge, draw a line starting at the '0' mark of the ruler and ending at the given length.

a) Draw a line 16 mm long.

b) Draw a line 41 mm long.

4. Estimate if each line is <u>less</u> or <u>more</u> than 30 mm long. Put a check in the appropriate column.

	Less than 30 mm	More than 30 mm
a) 		
b)		
c)		
d)		
e)		

5. How good were your estimates? Measure the length of each line in Question 4.

a) _____ mm   b) _____ mm   c) _____ mm   d) _____ mm   e) _____ mm

6. **Estimate** if the distance between the lines is <u>less</u> than 20 mm or <u>more</u> than 20 mm. Then measure the **actual** distance in millimetres.

	Less than 20 mm	More than 20 mm	Actual Distance
a) | |			
b) | |			
c) | |			
d) | |			

7. Measure the following lines in centimetres and millimetres.

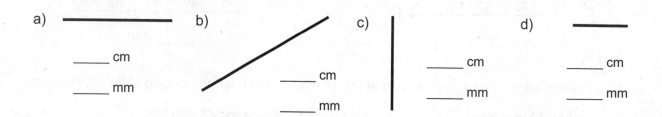

a) _____ cm _____ mm

b) _____ cm _____ mm

c) _____ cm _____ mm

d) _____ cm _____ mm

8. Measure the sides of the rectangles in cm. Then measure the distance between the two diagonal corners in cm and mm. (The dotted line is a guide for your ruler.)

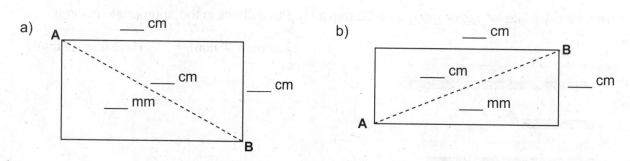

a) _____ cm, _____ cm, _____ mm, _____ cm

b) _____ cm, _____ cm, _____ mm, _____ cm

9. Use a ruler to draw the following objects to the exact millimetre.

    a) Draw a line 20 mm long.   b) Draw a line 27 mm long.   c) Draw a line 52 mm long.

    d) Draw a beetle 30 mm long.   e) Draw a pencil 70 mm long.   f) Draw a bicycle 28 mm long.

10. On grid paper, draw a rectangle with a length of 60 mm and a width of 2 cm.

ME4-6: Comparing Centimetres and Millimetres

1. How many millimetres (mm) are there in one centimetre (cm)? _____

2. To change a measurement from centimetres (cm) to millimetres (mm) what number do you have to multiply by? _____

3. Fill in the numbers missing from the following tables.

mm	cm
	4
57	
	5

mm	cm
	7
	12
35	

mm	cm
	112
	170
293	

mm	cm
	8
257	
	32

4. To change a measurement from mm to cm what number do you have to divide by? _____

   a) $40 \div 10 =$ _____   b) $60 \div 10 =$ _____   c) $2100 \div 10 =$ _____   d) $90 \div 10 =$ _____

   e) 320 mm = _____ cm   f) 30 mm = _____ cm   g) 910 mm = _____ cm   h) 650 mm = _____ cm

5. Fill in the following tables.

mm	cm
5	
	80

mm	cm
19	
1	

mm	cm
12	
	180

mm	cm
7	
	91

6. Convert the measurement in cm to mm (show your work). Then circle the greater measurement.

   a)   5 cm   70 mm   b)   83 cm   910 mm   c)   45 cm   53 mm

   d)   2 cm   12 mm   e)   60 cm   6200 mm   f)   72 cm   420 mm

7. Estimate the width and length (in cm) of each rectangle.
   Then measure each quantity exactly (in mm) with a ruler.

   a) [   ]   b) [   ]

   Estimate: _____ cm by _____ cm   Estimate: _____ cm by _____ cm

   Actual: _____ mm by _____ mm   Actual: _____ mm by _____ mm

1. Using a ruler, draw a second line so that the pair of lines are separated by the distance given. Then complete the chart.

		Distance apart	
		in cm	in mm
a)		4	40
b)		3	
c)			80
d)		7	

2. In the space provided, draw a line with a length between …

   a) 3 and 4 cm.   How long is your line in mm? _____

   b) 4 and 5 cm.   How long is your line in mm? _____

   c) 5 and 6 cm.   How long is your line in mm? _____

3. Write a measurement in mm that is between …

   a) 6 and 7 cm _____   b) 7 and 8 cm _____   c) 12 and 13 cm _____

4. Write a measurement in cm that is between …

   a) 67 mm and 75 mm _____   b) 27 mm and 39 mm _____

   c) 52 mm and 7 cm _____   d) 112 mm and 13 cm _____

5. Draw a line that is a whole number of centimetres and is between …

   a) 45 and 55 mm long.

   b) 65 and 75 mm long.

   c) 17 and 23 mm long.

6. Peter says 5 mm are longer than 2 cm because 5 is greater than 2.
   Is he right?
   Explain.

ME4-8: Problems and Puzzles

1. Each leaf has a different length.

Elm: 4 cm   Maple: 5 cm   Willow: 6 cm   Oak: 7 cm

Measure the lengths to identify each leaf.

_____

2. Which line is longer, A or B?

a)

A

B

b)

A

B

c)

A

B

A **metre** (m) is a unit of measurement for **length** (or **height** or **thickness**) equal to 100 cm.

A metre stick is 100 cm long.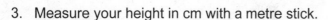

You can estimate metres using parts of your body.

- A giant step is about a metre long.
- A four- or five-year-old child is about a metre tall.
- If you stretch your arms out the distance between the tips of your fingers is about one metre. This distance is called your *arm span*.

1. Take a giant step and ask a friend to measure your step with a piece of string.
   Hold the string up to a metre stick.

   Is your step more or less than a metre? _____

2. Ask a friend to measure your arm span with a piece of string.

   Is your arm span more or less than a metre? _____

3. Measure your height in cm with a metre stick.

   Your height is _____ cm.   Are you taller than 1 metre? _____

4. Estimate the following distances.
   Then measure the actual distance with a metre stick or measuring tape.

   a) The length of a blackboard is ...   Estimate - ____ m _____ cm   Actual - ____ m _____ cm

   b) The length of your desk is ...   Estimate - ____ m _____ cm   Actual - ____ m _____ cm

   c) The distance from the floor to the door handle is ...   Estimate - ____ m _____ cm

   Actual - ____ m _____ cm

5. A small city block is about 100 m long.
   Write the name of a place you can walk to from your school
   (a store, a park, your house).

   Approximately, how far away from the school is the place you named?

ME4-10: Metres (Advanced)

1. Can you figure out the pattern in the following table and then finish it on your own?

m	1	2	3	4	5	6
dm	10	20				
cm	100	200				
mm	1000	2000				

2. a) 1 cm = _____ mm   b) 1 m = _____ cm   c) 1 m = _____ mm

3. Convert the following measurements.

a)
m	cm
1	
14	
80	

b)
m	mm
2	
19	
21	

c)
cm	mm
3	
65	
106	

4. Sheena measured the height of her bedroom window with both a metre stick and a measuring tape.
   - When she measured with the metre stick, the window was 2 m with 15 cm extra.
   - When she measured with the measuring tape, the measurement was 215 cm.

   Is there a difference in the two measurements? Explain.

   _____

   _____

5. Convert the measurements given in cm to measurements using multiple units.

   a) 513 cm = __5__ m __13__ cm   b) 217 cm = _____ m _____ cm

   c) 367 cm = _____ m _____ cm   d) 481 cm = _____ m _____ cm

   e) 706 cm = _____ m _____ cm   f) 303 cm = _____ m _____ cm

6. Convert the multiple-unit measurements to single-unit measurements.

   a) 3 m 71 cm = __371__ cm   b) 4 m 51 cm = _____ cm   c) 3 m 45 cm = _____ cm

   d) 8 m 2 cm = _____ cm   e) 9 m 7 cm = _____ cm   f) 7 m 50 cm = _____ cm

A **kilometre** is a unit of measurement for **length** equal to 1 000 metres.

1. a) Count by 100s to find out how many times you need to add 100 to make 1 000.

    100 , _____ , _____ , _____ , _____ , _____ , _____ , _____ , _____ , _____

    b) A football field is about 100 m long.
        How many football fields long is a kilometre?

    _____

2. a) Skip count by 50s to find out how many times you need to add 50 to make 1 000.

    __50__ , _____ , _____ , _____ , _____ , _____ , _____ , _____ , _____ , _____ .

    _____ , _____ , _____ , _____ , _____ , _____ , _____ , _____ , _____ , _____

    b) An Olympic swimming pool is 50 m long.
        How many swimming pools long is a kilometre?

    _____

3. Count by 10s to find the number of times you need to add 10 to make each number.

    a) 100 = _____ tens   b) 200 = _____ tens   c) 300 = _____ tens

    d) 400 = _____ tens   e) 500 = _____ tens   f) 600 = _____ tens

4. Using the pattern in Question 3, how many times would you need to add 10 to make 1 000?

    _____

5. A school bus is about 10 m long. How many school buses lined end to end will equal ...

    a) close to a kilometre? _____   b) close to 2 km? _____

6. You can travel 1 km if you walk for 15 minutes at a regular speed. Name a place (a store, a park, your friend's house) that is about 1 km from your school.

    _____

ME4-12: Kilometres and Metres

The number beside each bold line on the map indicates the length of the road (in kilometres) between the cities.

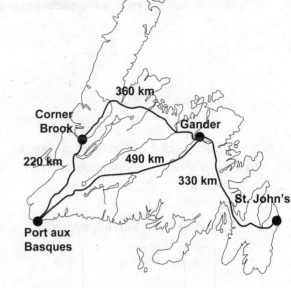

Newfoundland

1. The driving distance between …

   a) Corner Brook and Port aux Basques is _____ km.

   b) Corner Brook and Gander is _____ km.

   c) Port aux Basques and Gander is _____ km.

   d) Gander and St. John's is _____ km.

2. How far would you travel if you drove from …

   a) Corner Brook to Port aux Basques to Gander? _____ km

   b) Port aux Basques to Gander to St. John's? _____ km

   c) St. John's to Gander to Corner Brook? _____ km

3. Order the Canadian rivers from longest (1) to shortest (5).

River	Length
Clearwater (Sask.)	187 km
Bloodvein (Man.)	200 km
Kicking Horse (B.C.)	67 km
Jacques-Cartier (Que.)	128 km
Athabasca (Alta.)	168 km

1. _____

2. _____

3. _____

4. _____

5. _____

4. A track is 400 m long.

   a) If Khalid runs two times around the track, how many metres will he travel?

   b) Will he have travelled a km?

   c) Khalid plans to run a 1500 m race. About how many times must he run around the track?

   d) How many times must Khalid run around the track to cover 2 km?

For the questions below, you will need to choose the appropriate unit of measurement.
REMEMBER: You can refer to the guidelines provided.

| The thickness of a dime is about **1 mm**. | The width of your index finger is about **1 cm**. | The width of your hand is about **1 cm**. | The height of a 4- or 5-year-old child is about **1 m**. | The distance you can walk in 15 min is about **1 km**. |

1. Match the word with the symbol.

a)
| cm | metre |
| m | centimetre |

b)
cm	centimetre
m	kilometre
km	metre

c)
mm	kilometre
km	centimetre
cm	millimetre

2. Match the most appropriate unit of measurement with the object.

a)
| metre | height of a child |
| centimetre | length of a nail |

b)
metre	length of a worm
kilometre	height of a door
centimetre	length of a subway track

3. Match the word with the symbol. Then match the most appropriate unit of measurement with the object.

a)
mm	kilometre	book
cm	centimetre	length of a street
m	millimetre	height of the classroom
km	metre	length of an ant

b)
km	metre	door
cm	millimetre	distance to Montreal
m	kilometre	pencil
mm	centimetre	postage stamp

4. Order the following items from shortest to longest (1 = shortest, 2 = next shortest, 3 = longest). What unit would you use to measure each?

a)

\# ___   # ___   # ___

Unit: _____   Unit: _____   Unit: _____

b)

\# ___   # ___   # ___

Unit: _____   Unit: _____   Unit: _____

1. How many centimetres are in a metre? _____

2. Convert the following measurements into centimetres.

   a) 4 m = _____ cm   b) 6 m = _____ cm   c) _____ cm = 1 m   d) 3 m = _____ cm

3. Circle the greater amount.

   HINT: Convert the measurement in metres (m) to centimetres (cm) first. Show your work in the box provided.

   a) 1 m   or   60 cm

   _____ cm

   b) 7 m   or   82 cm

   _____ cm

   c) 410 cm   or   5 m

   _____ cm

   d) 3 m   or   340 cm

   _____ cm

   e) 280 cm   or   4 m

   _____ cm

   f) 7 m   or   680 cm

   _____ cm

4. Mark the measurements on the number line. (First convert all measurements to cm.)

   A.   150 cm

   B.   2 m

   C.   1 m

0 cm	50 cm	100 cm	150 cm	200 cm

5. This table shows the lengths
   of some animals at the zoo.

Snake	Length
Lynx - **L**	150 cm
Rabbit - **R**	50 cm
Beaver - **B**	100 cm
Wolf - **W**	2 m

   Mark the lengths of **L**, **R**, **B** and **W** on the number line.

0 cm	100 cm	200 cm

1. Which is the best unit of measurement for …

    a) the length of a chalkboard eraser?

    _____

    b) the length of a subway car?

    _____

    c) the distance travelled on a flight from Halifax to Moncton? Explain.

    _____

    _____

2. Which unit of measurement will make the statement correct?

    a) The thickness of a piece of construction paper is about 1 _____ .

    b) Schools might close if more than 50 _____ of snow fell overnight.

    c) An average adult bicycle is about 2 _____ long.

    d) It is more than 500 _____ from Toronto to Montreal.

    e) The classroom door is about 2 _____ high.

    f) Your shoe is close to 15 _____ long.

    g) The CN Tower is about 553 _____ high.

3. What would you use to measure the following distances: metres (m) or kilometres (km)? Explain one of your answers below.

    a) From your class to the cafeteria: _____   b) From your home to school: _____

    c) Between Toronto and Ottawa: _____   d) Around the school yard: _____

    _____

    _____

4. Some BIG and SMALL facts about Canada!
   Complete each sentence with the appropriate unit of measurement (km, m or cm).
   TEACHER: Read these questions out loud to your students before assigning the exercise.

   a) The Red Deer River flows from Alberta to Saskatchewan.

   It is 724 _____ long.

   b) The city of Stewart, British Columbia gets a lot of snowfall.

   It receives about 660 _____ of snowfall every year.

   c) The CN Tower, at 553 _____, is North America's tallest free-standing structure.

   d) The Douglas Fir tree can grow to a height of 100 _____.

   e) An Atlantic Cod is about 1 _____ long and can swim in water that is 305 _____ deep.

   f) The width of a maple leaf is approximately 16 _____.

5. Which unit of measurement would you use for the following?

   a) Length of a postage stamp:

   _____

   b) Distance from your home to school:

   _____

   c) Length of a subway car:

   _____

   d) Length of your hair:

   _____

   e) Distance travelled on a flight from Halifax to Moncton:

   _____

6. Choose any object in your classroom.
   Which unit of measurement would be best to measure the object?
   Explain.

Maria made this figure with toothpicks.

She then counted the number of toothpicks around the outside of the figure.

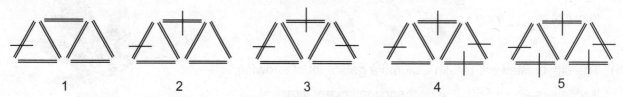

1   2   3   4   5

The distance around the outside of a shape is called the **perimeter** of the shape. The perimeter of Maria's figure, measured in toothpicks, is five toothpicks.

---

1. Count the number of toothpicks around the outside of the figure. (Mark the toothpicks as you count so you don't miss any!) Write your answer in the circle provided.

a)  ○   b)  ○   c) 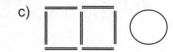 ○

2. Count the number of edges around the <u>outside</u> of the figure, marking the edges as you count.

 } edge

a)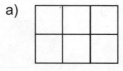

b)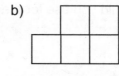

c)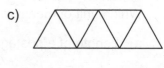

_____   _____   _____

3. Each edge is 1 cm long. Find the perimeter in cm.

a)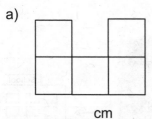

_____ cm

b)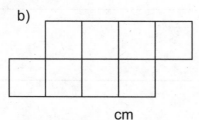

_____ cm

c)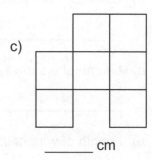

_____ cm

4. The pictures show the designs for two gardens. Find the perimeter of each garden by writing an addition statement.

a)

_____

b)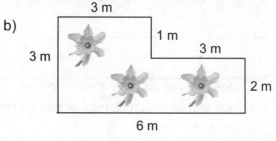

_____

5. Write the perimeter of each figure in the sequence (assume each edge is 1 unit).

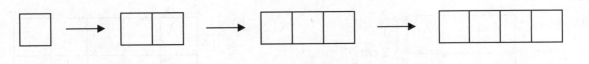

_____   _____   _____   _____

a) How does the perimeter change each time a square is added?

_____

b) What will the perimeter of the 6th figure be? _____

6. Write the perimeter of each figure in the sequence below.

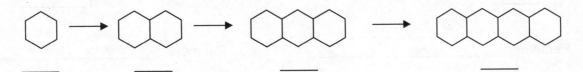

_____   _____   _____   _____

a) How does the perimeter change each time a hexagon is added?

_____

b) What will the perimeter of the 6th figure be? _____

7. a) Perimeter: _____

Add one square so that
the perimeter of the figure
increases by 2.

New Perimeter: _____

b) Perimeter: _____

Add one square so that
the perimeter of the figure
stays the same.

New Perimeter: _____

8. The pictures (**A** and **B**) show two ways to make a rectangle using four squares.

a) Which figure has the shorter perimeter? How do you know?

b) Are there any other ways to make a rectangle using 4 squares?

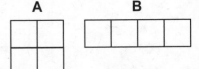

9. On grid paper, show all the ways you can make a rectangle using …

a) 6 squares.   b) 10 squares.   c) 9 squares.

1. Each edge is 1 cm long. Write the total length of each side beside the figure (one side is done for you). Then write an addition statement and find the perimeter.

a)

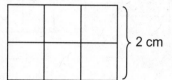

Perimeter: _____

b)

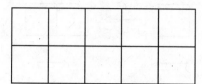

Perimeter: _____

c)

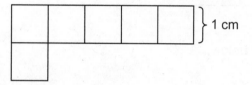

Perimeter: _____

d)

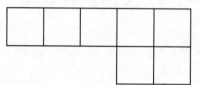

Perimeter: _____

2. Each edge is 1 unit long. Write the length of each side beside the figure (don't miss any edges!). Then use the side lengths to find the perimeter.

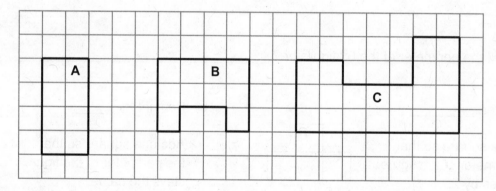

3. Draw your own figure and find its perimeter.

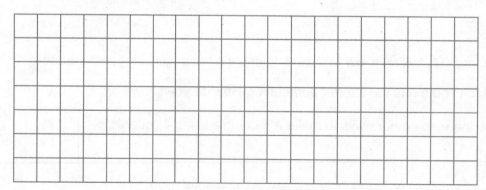

4. On grid paper, draw your own figures and find their perimeters. Try drawing letters or other shapes!

ME4-18: Measuring Perimeter

1. Measure the perimeter of each figure in cm using a ruler.

   a)

   b)

   c)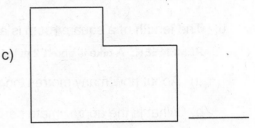

2. a) Find the perimeter of each figure (include the units).

   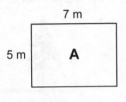 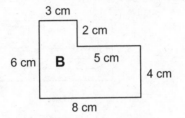 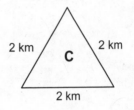 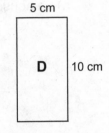

   Perimeter: _____   Perimeter: _____   Perimeter: _____   Perimeter: _____

   b) Write the letters of the figures in order from greatest to least perimeter. Watch the units!

   _____ , _____ , _____ , _____

3. Estimate the perimeter of each figure in cm. Then measure the actual perimeter with a ruler.

   a)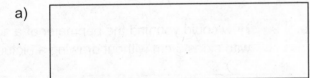

   b)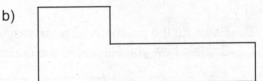

   Estimated Perimeter: _____   Estimated Perimeter: _____

   Actual Perimeter: _____   Actual Perimeter: _____

4. Estimate the perimeter of your JUMP workbook in cm. Then measure the perimeter with a ruler.
   HINT: The width of your hand, with your fingers spread slightly, is about 10 cm.

   Estimated Perimeter: _____   Actual Perimeter: _____

5. a) About how many bicycles, parked end to end, would fit along the width of your classroom?

   b) A bicycle is about 2 metres long. About how many metres wide is your classroom?

   c) About how many metres long is your classroom?

   d) What is the approximate perimeter of your classroom?

Measurement 1

6. The length of a square room is about $3\frac{1}{2}$ bicycles.

   REMEMBER: A bike is about 2 m long.

   a) About how many metres long is the room? _____

   b) What is the approximate perimeter of the room? _____

7. What unit (cm, m or km) would you use to measure the perimeter of ...

   a) a house? _____   b) a book? _____   c) a school yard? _____   d) a provincial park? _____

           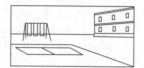

   e) a calculator? _____   f) a city? _____   g) a basketball court? _____   h) a country? _____

          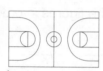   

8. Estimate the perimeter of a room in your home. Explain how you estimated the perimeter.

9. How could you find the perimeter of a square with sides 5 cm without drawing a picture?

10. Sally arranged four squares (each with sides 1 m) to make a poster.

    1 m {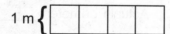

    She wants to make a border for her poster out of ribbon.

    Ribbon costs 15¢ for each metre.
    How much will the border cost?

11. How could you measure the perimeter of a round object (like a plate or a can) using a strip of paper and a ruler?

12. Explain the meaning of perimeter.

13. Can two different shapes have the same perimeter?

    Explain your thinking on grid paper.

ME4-19: Telling Time (Review)

1. How many minutes is it past the hour? Count by 5s around the clock, filling in the boxes as you go.

a)

b)

c)

d)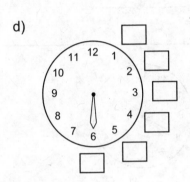

e)

f)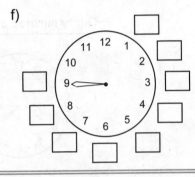

2. What is the hour?
   The first one has been done for you.

Example:

The hour hand (the short hand) moves in a clockwise direction.
When the hand is between 7 and 8 **the hour is still 7**.

a)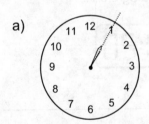

Hour: ___1___

b)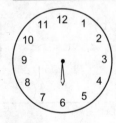

Hour: _____

c)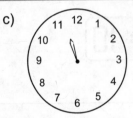

Hour: _____

d)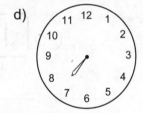

Hour: _____

e)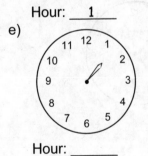

Hour: _____

f)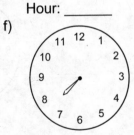

Hour: _____

g)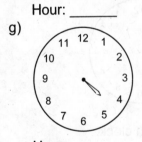

Hour: _____

h)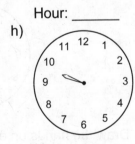

Hour: _____

i)

Hour: _____

j)

Hour: _____

k)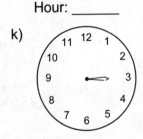

Hour: _____

l)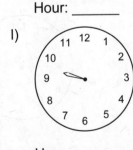

Hour: _____

jump math
MULTIPLYING POTENTIAL

Measurement 1

3. Give the time on the following analog clocks: (i) in numbers; and (ii) in words.

a)

<u>12</u> : <u>30</u>

Thirty minutes after twelve

b)

_____ : _____

_____

c)

_____ : _____

_____

d)

_____ : _____

_____

4. Give the time on the following digital clocks in: (i) in words; and (ii) as an analog clock.

a)

_____

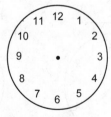

b)

_____

5. Draw the hands on each clock.

a)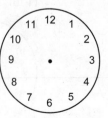

4:45

b)

8:15

c)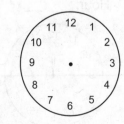

2:10

ME4-20: Telling Time (Half and Quarter Hours)

When the minute hand (the long hand) travels from the 12 around the clock until it hits the 12 again, **one hour** has passed.

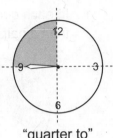
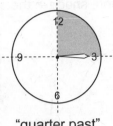

"half past"   "quarter past"   "quarter to"

---

1. In each question, shade in the space from the 12 to the minute hand as above. Then indicate whether the minute hand is "half past", "quarter past" or "quarter to" the hour.

a)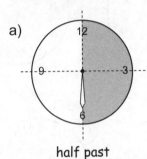

half past

b)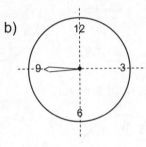

c)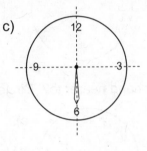

d)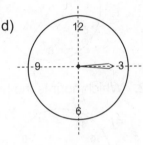

e)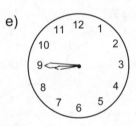

f)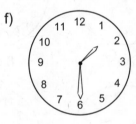

g)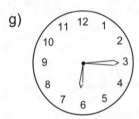

h)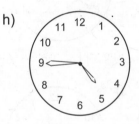

2. Circle the right answer. The first one has been done for you.

a)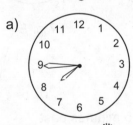

quarter to 8 or 7

b)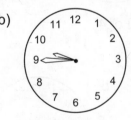

quarter to 10 or 9

c)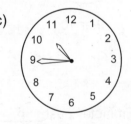

quarter to 10 or 11

d)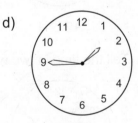

quarter to 1 or 2

e)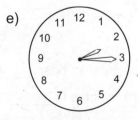

quarter past 2 or 3

f)

quarter past 4 or 5

g)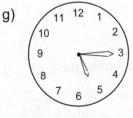

quarter past 5 or 6

h)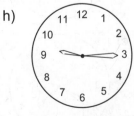

quarter past 10 or 9

ME4-21: Telling Time in Two Ways

1. In each question, shade in the spaces from the 12 to the minute hand, so that the shaded part is less than a half.

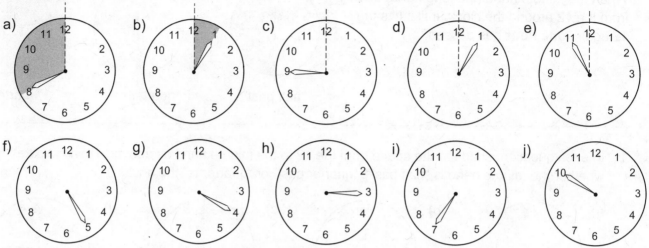

2. Which hour is the hour hand nearer to? Circle the right answer.

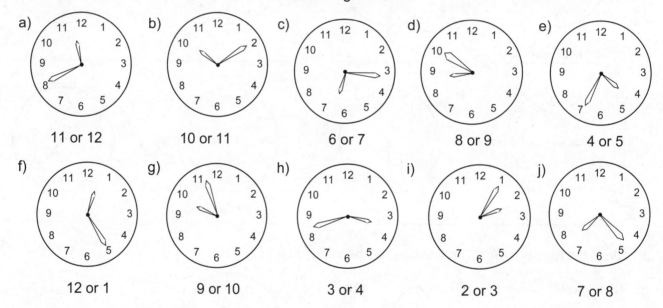

a) 11 or 12   b) 10 or 11   c) 6 or 7   d) 8 or 9   e) 4 or 5

f) 12 or 1   g) 9 or 10   h) 3 or 4   i) 2 or 3   j) 7 or 8

3. Tell the time in two ways.

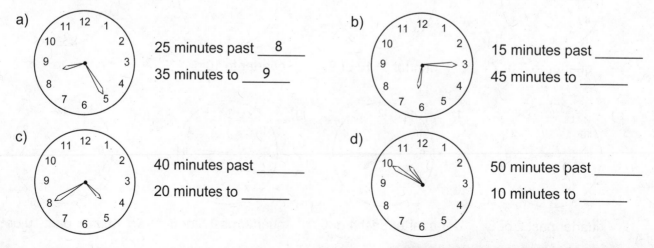

a) 25 minutes past ___8___
35 minutes to ___9___

b) 15 minutes past _____
45 minutes to _____

c) 40 minutes past _____
20 minutes to _____

d) 50 minutes past _____
10 minutes to _____

jump math
MULTIPLYING POTENTIAL

Measurement 1

ME4-22: Telling Time (One-Minute Intervals)

Each division on the clock stands for 1 minute.

When we count, we can see that the minute hand is pointing three lines (or 3 minutes) after the 12.

This means that it is **three minutes after the hour.**

Example:
On this clock, the minute hand is pointing between the 4 and the 5.

First we count by 5's until we reach the 4: 20 minutes have passed.
Then we count on by ones: 2 minutes have passed.

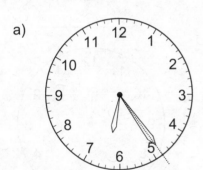

$$20 + 2 = 22 \text{ minutes have passed}$$

It is **2:22** or **twenty-two minutes after two.**

----

1. How many minutes past the hour is it? The first one has been done for you.

a)

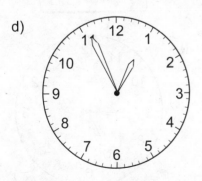

___24___ minutes past

b)

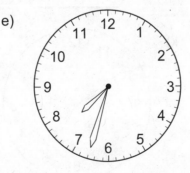

_____ minutes past

c)

_____ minutes past

d)

_____ minutes past

e)

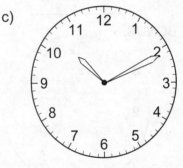

_____ minutes past

f)

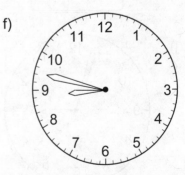

_____ minutes past

Measurement 1

2. For each clock, write the entire time – that is, the hour and the exact minute. The first one has been done for you.

a)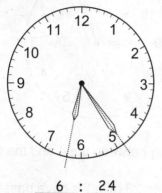

<u> 6 </u> : <u> 24 </u>

b)

_____ : _____

c)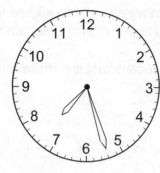

_____ : _____

d)

_____ : _____

e)

_____ : _____

f)

_____ : _____

BONUS:

g)

h)

i)

j)

k)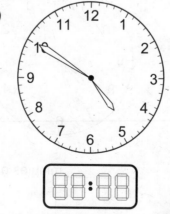

l)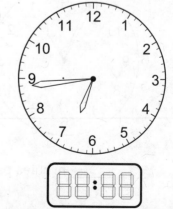

ME4-23: Elapsed Time

1. By counting by 5s, find out how much time elapsed from…

a)

Start time

End time

5:10 to 5:30

_____

b)
3:05 to 3:35

_____

c)
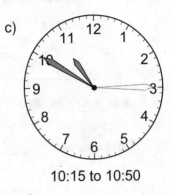
10:15 to 10:50

_____

d)
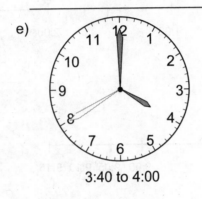
7:35 to 8:00

_____

e)
3:40 to 4:00

_____

f)

9:25 to 10:00

_____

2. Count by 5s to show how much time has elapsed between …

a) 6:50 and 7:25.

  __6:50__ , __6:55__ , __7:00__ , __7:05__ , _____, _____, _____, _____, _____
     0   5   10   15

Time elapsed: _____

b) 4:45 and 5:05.

  _____, _____, _____, _____, _____, _____, _____, _____, _____

Time elapsed: _____

c) 12:35 and 1:05.

  _____, _____, _____, _____, _____, _____, _____, _____, _____

Time elapsed: _____

d) 1:55 and 2:30.

  _____, _____, _____, _____, _____, _____, _____, _____, _____

Time elapsed: _____

3. It is now 5:10. Mohamed started playing at 4:25. How long has he been playing?

4. Kyla goes to bed at 7:45. Jake's bed time is 30 minutes later. What time does Jake go to bed?

5. Ann put cookies in the oven at 4:50. They should bake for 40 minutes.
   At what time should she take them out?

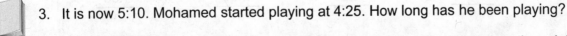

jump math
MULTIPLYING POTENTIAL

Measurement 1

1. Find how much time has passed between the times in bold (intervals are not shown to scale).

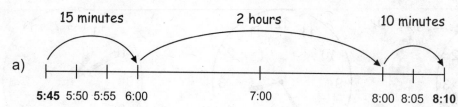

a)

15 minutes   2 hours   10 minutes

5:45 5:50 5:55 6:00   7:00   8:00 8:05 8:10

Time elapsed: _____

b)

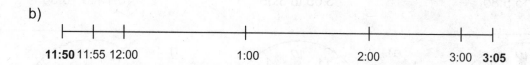

11:50 11:55 12:00   1:00   2:00   3:00 3:05

Time elapsed: _____

c)

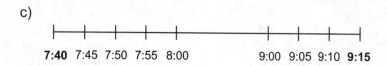

7:40 7:45 7:50 7:55 8:00   9:00 9:05 9:10 9:15

Time elapsed: _____

2. Count on by 5-minute and by 1-hour intervals to find out how much time has elapsed between ...

a) 3:45 and 6:05.

    3:45 , 3:50 , 3:55 , 4:00 , 5:00 , 6:00 , 6:05   Time elapsed: _____

b) 7:50 and 9:10.

    _____, _____, _____, _____, _____, _____, _____   Time elapsed: _____

c) 10:55 and 12:20.

    _____, _____, _____, _____, _____, _____, _____   Time elapsed: _____

3. Find how much time has elapsed by subtraction.

a)   3:43   b)   8:22   c)   11:48   d)   6:40   e)   3:42
    − 3:20   − 7:21   − 5:30   − 2:25   − 1:05
    _____   _____   _____   _____   _____

4. Draw a time line to find out how much time has elapsed between ...

a) 7:40 and 10:10.   b) 4:35 and 6:05.   c) 8:50 and 10:10.

ME4-25: Times of Day

The time period from **12 o'clock midnight** to **12 o'clock noon** is called **a.m.**

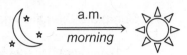

a.m.
morning

Example: When you wake up at **7 o'clock in the morning**, it is called **7 a.m.**

The time period from **12 o'clock noon** to **12 o'clock midnight** is called **p.m.**

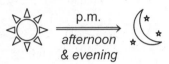

p.m.
afternoon
& evening

Example: When you go to bed at **8 o'clock in the evening**, it is called **8 p.m.**

----

1. Are the following times **a.m.** or **p.m.**?

   a) 7 o'clock in the morning _____

   b) 2 o'clock in the afternoon _____

   c) 9 o'clock in the evening _____

   d) 10 o'clock at night _____

   e) 4 o'clock in the afternoon _____

   f) 3 o'clock in the morning _____

   BONUS:

   g) 2 hours <u>before</u> noon _____

   h) 3 hours <u>after</u> noon _____

   i) 1 hour <u>before</u> midnight _____

   j) 4 hours <u>after</u> midnight _____

2. a) List two things you do in the **a.m.**

   b) List two things you do in the **p.m.**

3. Anit's schedule:

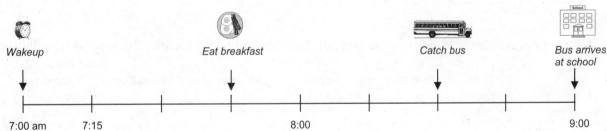

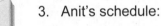

| Wakeup | Eat breakfast | Catch bus | Bus arrives at school |

7:00 am   7:15   8:00   9:00

   a) At what time does Anit eat breakfast?

   b) What time does he catch the bus?

   c) How long does the bus take to get to school?

4. Design a time line of a typical school day. Include the time you wake up, leave for school, etc.

ME4-26: The 24-Hour Clock

1. Complete the following table using the pattern.

12-hr Clock	24-hr Clock
12:00 a.m.	00:00
1:00 a.m.	01:00
2:00 a.m.	02:00

12-hr Clock	24-hr Clock
9:00 a.m.	09:00
10:00 a.m.	
12:00 p.m.	12:00
1 p.m.	13:00

12-hr Clock	24-hr Clock
5:00 p.m.	17:00
6:00 p.m.	

2. a) What number must you add to 1 p.m. to change it to 24-hour clock notation? _____

   b) List three other times that change this way: _____

3. For each a.m./p.m. time, write the corresponding 24-hour clock notation.
   HINT: Only look at the chart above if you need help.

   a) 5:00 a.m. = _____   b) 11:00 p.m. = _____   c) 6:00 p.m. = _____

   d) 3:00 p.m. = _____   e) 8:00 p.m. = _____   f) 12:00 a.m. = _____

   g) 12:00 p.m. = _____   h) 9:00 p.m. = _____

4. For each 24-hour clock notation, write the corresponding a.m./p.m. time.

   a) 07:00 = _____   b) 15:00 = _____   c) 13:00 = _____   d) 00:00 = _____

   e) 18:00 = _____   f) 17:00 = _____   g) 06:00 = _____   h) 23:00 = _____

5. Complete the chart to show when David left each section of the museum (using 24-hour time).

	Start	Dinosaurs	Reptiles	Lunch	Ancient Egypt	Bat Cave
Time Spent		1 hour	2 hour	30 minutes	1 hour	30 minutes
Time Finished	10:30					

6. Describe any differences between the way time is written for a 24-hr and a 12-hr clock …

   a) in the morning (a.m.).   b) in the afternoon or evening (p.m.).

ME4-27: Time Intervals

1. Change the time expressed in weeks and days to days only.

    a) 2 weeks 3 days

    = __14__ days + __3__ days

    = __17__ days

    b) 2 weeks 5 days

    = ____ days + ____ days

    = ____ days

    c) 3 weeks 2 days

    = ____ days + ____ days

    = _____ days

2. Janice wants to know how long it took her plant to grow a certain height. Help her find the time in days.

Height of Janice's plant	Time after Planting (in weeks and days)	Rough Work	Time after Planting (in days)
2 cm	0 weeks and 4 days	0 × 7 = 0 0 + 4 = 4	4
4 cm	1 week and 1 day	1 × 7 = 7 7 + 1 = 8	
6 cm	1 week and 5 days		
8 cm	2 weeks and 2 days		
10 cm	2 weeks and 6 days		
12 cm	3 weeks and 3 days		

    a) Complete the chart.

    b) How long does it take for the plant to grow 2 cm? _____

    c) Looking at the chart, how long (in days) would you guess it took for the plant to reach 11 cm?

3. Approximately how long does it take you to perform the following activities? Don't forget units!

Activity	Estimated Daily Time
Sleeping	
Getting dressed	
Getting to school	
Eating lunch	
Doing homework	

Activity	Estimated Daily Time
Playing outside	
Reading	
Talking to your family	
Watching TV	
Daydreaming	

ME4-28: Longer Time Intervals

Years are related to days and weeks as follows:

1 year = 365 days   and   **1 year = 52 weeks**

NOTE: There are 366 days in a leap year.

----

1. Put the units in order from smallest to largest (1 means smallest; 5 means largest).

day	minute	week	year	hour
	1			

2. Fill in the charts.

a)

Days	Hours
1	24
2	
3	

b)

Weeks	Days
1	7
2	
3	

c)

Years	Weeks
1	52
2	
3	

d)

Years	Days
1	365
2	
3	

3. Match each question with the unit of time you would use to give the answer.

How old are you?   months

How long does recess last?   years

How long do you sleep each night?   weeks

How long is March Break?   minutes

How long is summer vacation?   hours

4.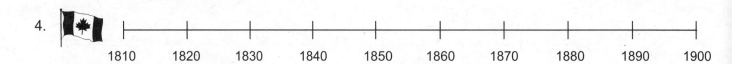

Sir John A. Macdonald was the first Prime Minister of Canada.

a) Mark the events from his life on the time line.

b) How old was he when he moved to Canada?

_____

c) How long after he moved to Canada did Canada become a country?

_____

A	1815	Born in Scotland
B	1820	Moved to Canada
C	1843	Married Isabella Clark
D	1867	Canada became a country
E	1891	Died in Ottawa

ME4-29: Topics in Time

1. Unscramble the months and write them in order.

    June, February, April, January, December, May, March, November, August, October, July, September

    1. _____   2. _____   3. _____   4. _____

    5. _____   6. _____   7. _____   8. _____

    9. _____   10. _____   11. _____   12. _____

2. Give the numbers of each month.
    NOTE: Put a 0 in front of 1-digit numbers.
    For instance write May as 05.

Month	Number
April	
February	
December	

3. Convert the dates below into standard (SI) notation.

    a) June 18, 1963

    _____

    b) April 9, 1976

    _____

    Example:
    June 5, 2002
    2002 – 06 – 05

    c) May 24, 2001

    _____

    d) December 25, 1987

    _____

    e) September 29, 1942

    _____

    f) July 1, 1867

    _____

    g) March 14, 1973

    _____

4. Convert the following dates into written form.

    a) 1982 – 07 – 25 _____   b) 1999 – 12 – 31 _____

    c) 2001 – 06 – 01 _____   d) 1963 – 05 – 07 _____

    e) 1977 – 05 – 17 _____   f) 1981 – 05 – 08 _____

5. A decade is 10 years. A century is 100 years. Fill in the blanks.

    a) 40 years = _____ decades   b) 60 years = _____ decades   c) 90 years = _____ decades

    d) 200 years = _____ centuries   e) 800 years = _____ centuries   f) 1500 years = _____ centuries

    g) 2 decades = _____ years   h) 3 centuries = _____ years   i) 40 decades = ____ centuries

6. Is the date 2003 – 24 – 02 possible in SI Notation? Explain. What error do you think was made

7. Canada became a country in 1867.   a) Was this more than a century ago?

    b) About how many decades ago was this?

jump math
MULTIPLYING POTENTIAL.

Measurement 1

Data is facts or information. For example, your age is a piece of data, and so is your name.

Data can be organized into **categories**. We use attributes to sort data, such as …

- Gender (boy or girl)
- Age (age 9 or age 10)
- Length of Hair (long hair or short hair)

----

1. *Animals:*   sparrow,   butterfly,   tuna,   hawk,

   shark,   beetle,   robin,   ant.

   a) Circle the animals that are birds.

   b) Underline the animals that are fish.

   c) How many animals are in each category?   Birds _____   Fish _____   Insects _____

2. Count how many are in each category.

   Foods: ham,   apple,   banana,   milk,   yogurt,

   strawberry,   cheese,   chicken,   grapes.

   Categories: Fruit _____   Meat _____   Dairy products _____

3. Match the data with the correct category.

   A. Toronto, Calgary, Halifax   _____ pizza toppings

   B. baseball, soccer, tennis   _____ coins

   C. cheese, pepperoni, mushrooms   _____ trees

   D. maple, oak, beech   _____ cities in Canada

   E. nickel, dime, quarter   _____ sports

4. Which category describes each group of numbers?

   a) 7, 9, 52, 11, 6, 33   ☐ greater than 4   ☐ 4 or less

   b) 19, 11, 3, 5, 21, 7   ☐ even numbers   ☐ odd numbers

   c) $\frac{1}{2}$, $\frac{3}{4}$, $\frac{1}{4}$, $\frac{2}{5}$, $\frac{5}{10}$ ☐ whole numbers   ☐ fractions

5. What attribute do you think was used to sort the data?   1, 5, 3, 7, 9   0, 2, 8, 4, 6

PDM4-2: Venn Diagrams

In math, we sometimes use circles to show which objects have a property.
Objects inside a circle have the property, and objects outside the circle do not.

---

1. Put the letters from each shape inside or outside the circle. The first one is done for you.

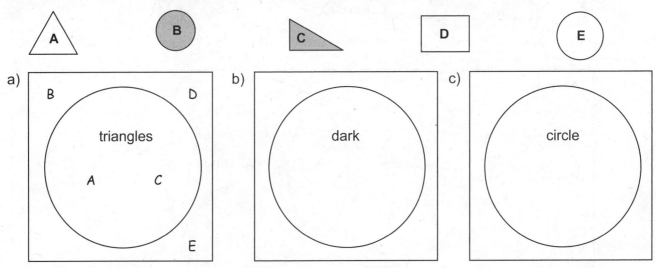

a)

B   D

triangles

A   C

E

b)

dark

c)

circle

2. We can organize the shapes above into circles at the same time. The overlapping circles are called a **Venn** diagram.

a) Shade the area that is **inside** both circles.
   Put the correct letter in that area.

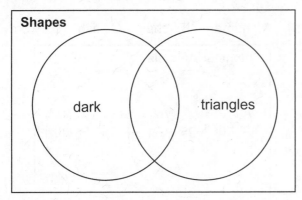

Shapes

dark   triangles

b) Shade the area that is **outside** both circles.
   Put the correct letter in that area.

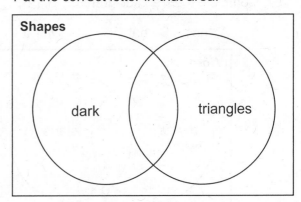

Shapes

dark   triangles

3. Complete the Venn diagrams.

a)

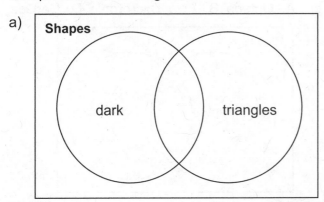

Shapes

dark   triangles

b)

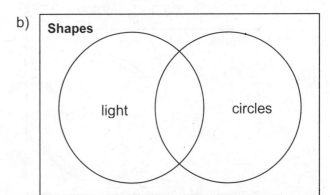

Shapes

light   circles

4. Complete the Venn diagram.

A. bat   B. dog   C. pigeon   D. cat   E. mosquito   F. ostrich   G. sparrow   H. bee

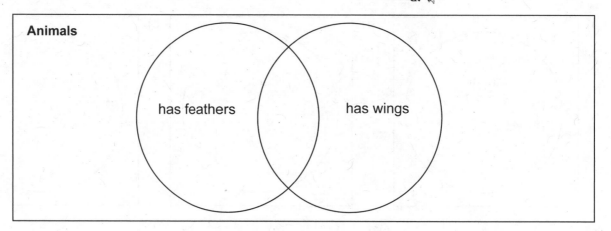

Animals

has feathers   has wings

One part of the Venn diagram is empty. Explain what that means: _____

_____

5. Complete the Venn diagrams.

a)   A. rice   B. hat   C. sit   D. rat

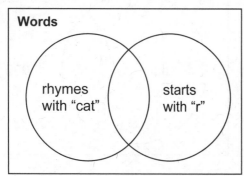

Words

rhymes with "cat"   starts with "r"

b)   A. human   B. chair   C. fish   D. worm

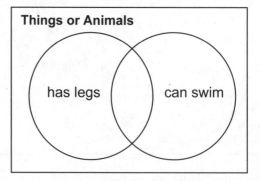

Things or Animals

has legs   can swim

c)   A. cat   B. listen   C. watch   D. fly

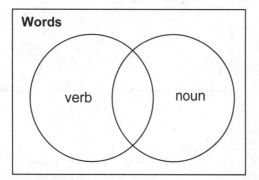

Words

verb   noun

c)   A. Ontario B. Asia C. Toronto D. Canada

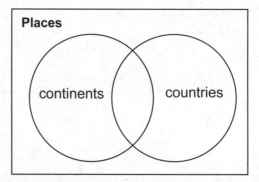

Places

continents   countries

1.  Bradley loves to learn about space. Using the Internet with help from his teacher, he collected the following information about the planets in our solar system:

NOTE: Hours are rounded to the nearest whole number.

Planet	Number of Moons	Hours Needed to Rotate on Axis
Mercury (A)	0	1416
Venus (B)	0	5832
Earth (C)	1	24
Mars (D)	2	25
Jupiter (E)	62	10
Saturn (F)	33	11
Uranus (G)	27	17
Neptune (H)	13	16

a) Which planets have fewer than 2 moons?

List their letters here: _____, _____, _____

b) Which planets take fewer than 100 hours to rotate once on their axis?

List their letters here: _____, _____, _____, _____, _____, _____

c) Are any planets on **both** lists? If so, circle this planet's letter in both the lists above.

d) Now place **all** the planets – by letter – into the Venn diagram.

Pay attention to the planet you have circled. Where will it go?

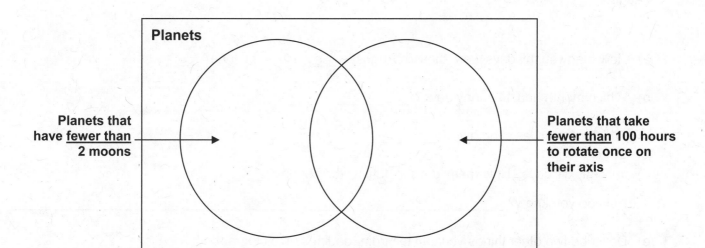

PDM4-4: Revisiting Pictographs

A **pictograph** uses a **symbol** to represent data.

Number of Books Read in December	
Josef	📖 📖 📖 📖 📖
Alexander	📖 📖 📖

The scale of the pictograph is the number of items each symbol represents.

A **key** tells what the scale is:

Number of Books Read in 1 Year	
Ravi	📖 📖 📖 📖 📖
Kamal	📖 📖 📖
	1 📖 means 10 books

OR

Key to the scale

Number of Books Read in 1 Year	
Ravi	📖 📖 📖 📖 📖 📖 📖 📖 📖 📖
Kamal	📖 📖 📖 📖 📖
	1 📖 means 5 books

---

1. Complete the pictograph.

SCALE: 1 ☼ = 2 days of sun

Month	Number of Sunny Days	Count # of Suns x 2 = # of Sunny Days
April	☼ ☼ ☼ ☼ ☼ ☼	6 x 2 = 12 sunny days in April
May	☼ ☼ ☼ ☼ ☼ ☼ ☼	
June	☼ ☼ ☼ ☼ ☼ ☼ ☼ ☼ ☼	
July	☼ ☼ ☼ ☼ ☼ ☼ ☼ ☼ ☼ ☼ ☼ ☼ ☼	
August	☼ ☼ ☼ ☼ ☼ ☼ ☼ ☼ ☼ ☼ ☼ ☼	

a) How many sunny days were there in August? _____   in June? _____

b) Which month had 14 sunny days? _____

c) Which month was sunniest? _____

d) July has 31 days. How many days in July *weren't* sunny? _____

   How do you know? _____

e) Describe two other things you can tell from reading this pictograph.

2. Count the tallies and complete the pictograph.

Your tally

Plant   **Number of Seeds**

Rose |||| |||| |||| |||| |||| |||| |||| |||| |||| |||| = _____ seeds

Dandelion |||| |||| |||| |||| = _____ seeds

Pansy |||| |||| = _____ seeds

Your pictograph

KEY: ⬭ = 10 seeds

Plant	Number of Seeds
Rose	
Dandelion	
Pansy	

3. There are three different colours of marbles: blue (B), green (G) and yellow (Y).

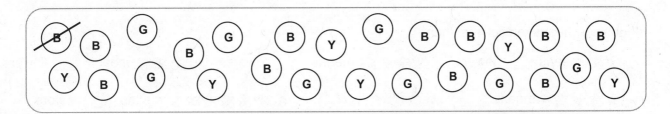

Tally the marbles (the first one has been started for you) and then complete the pictograph.

KEY: ⊙ = 2 marbles

Colour	Tally	Pictograph
Blue	|	
Green		
Yellow		

Manuel has counted the flowers in his garden.

Flower	Daffodil	Buttercup	Daisy
Number	15	25	40

He wants to display his data in a pictograph.

Here are two ways he could display his data, using a **scale**:

Number of Flowers

Daffodil   ❀ ❀ ❀

Buttercup   ❀ ❀ ❀ ❀ ❀

Daisy   ❀ ❀ ❀ ❀ ❀ ❀ ❀ ❀

Scale: One ❀ means 5 flowers

Number of Flowers

Daffodil   ◐◖

Buttercup   ◐◐◖

Daisy   ◐◐◐◐

Scale: One ◐ means 10 flowers

- -

1. In the pictograph above, Manual used a half cirlce. Circle the symbol that will work best if …

    a) You need half symbols.

    b) You need quarter symbols.

2. If one ◯ means two books, then …

    a) ◯◯◯ means ____ books.   b) ◯◯ means ____ books.   c) ◯◯◖ means ____ books.

    d) ◯◯◯◯◯◖ means ____ books.   e) ◯◯◯◯◯◯◖ means ____ books.

    If one ❀ means ten flowers, then …

    f) ❀❀ means ____ flowers.   g) ❀❀❀ means ____ flowers.   h) ❀❀❀ means ____ flowers.

    i) ❀❀❀❀❀ means ____ flowers.   j) ❀❀❀❀❀❀❀❀ means ____ flowers.

    If one ☺ means four tickets, then …

    k) ☺☺ means ____ tickets.   l) ☺☺☺ means ____ tickets.   m) ☺☺ means ____ tickets.

    n) ☺☺☺☺☺ means ____ tickets.   o) ☺☺☺☺☺☺ means ____ tickets.

3. Which scale works best with the data?

    a) 12, 6, 8   ☐ scale of 2   ☐ scale of 5   ☐ scale of 10

    b) 30, 90, 60   ☐ scale of 2   ☐ scale of 5   ☐ scale of 10

    c) 9, 12, 6   ☐ scale of 2   ☐ scale of 3   ☐ scale of 5

    d) 25, 10, 35   ☐ scale of 2   ☐ scale of 3   ☐ scale of 5

1. Theresa asked **20** of her classmates about their favourite type of book, but she forgot to include a scale in her pictograph.

My Classmates' Reading Preferences:	
Favourite Type of Book	**Number of Students**
Mysteries	📖 📖
Adventure	📖 📖 📖
Science Fiction	📖
Comic Books	📖 📖 📖
Magazines	📖

a) How many books are there in Theresa's pictograph altogether? _____

b) Does each book represent one student? Explain.

c) There are 20 students in Theresa's class. How many students do you think each book represents?

📖 = _____ students

d) Using the **scale** you found, calculate how many students preferred each type of book. Complete the chart.

   HINT: The total should be 20 students. If it isn't, try a different scale.

Favourite Type of Book	Number of Students
Mysteries	
Adventure	
Science Fiction	
Comic Books	
Magazines	

2. If there were 40 students in Theresa's class, then how many students would each book represent? Explain.

A **bar graph** has four parts:

- a vertical and horizontal **axis,**
- a **scale**,
- **labels** (including a title),
- and **data** (shown in bars).

The bars in a bar graph can be vertical or horizontal:

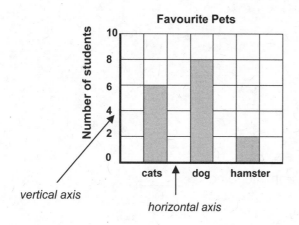

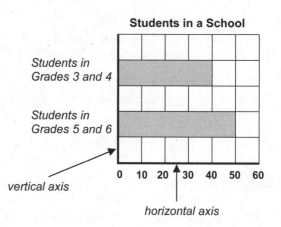

Bar graphs are drawn on **grids**. The labels tell what the data in the bar is. The scale tells how much each mark on the grid represents.

You can use the scale to determine what each bar represents.

---

1. a) How many students in Ms. Goodreau's class have …

    green eyes? _____   brown eyes? _____

    b) How many students have either brown or blue eyes? _____

    c) There are nine students in the class with hazel eyes. Colour the final bar in the graph to show this fact.

    d) How many students <u>don't</u> have hazel eyes? _____

    e) Altogether, how many students are there in Ms. Goodreau's class? _____

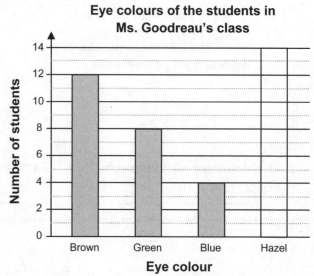

2. Anita did a survey of the different flowers in her school's front garden. Here are her results.

Flower type	Marigold	Sunflower	Tulip	Begonia
Tally	|||| |||| ||	||||	|||| |||	|||
Count				

a) Complete the "count" on Anita's tally chart.

b) Use Anita's tally chart to complete the bar graph below. Don't forget to give your graph a title!

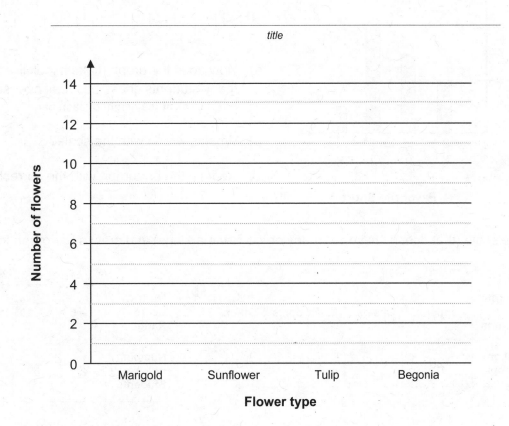

title

c) What are two conclusions that Anita can draw from her data?

- _____

- _____

1. The numbers on the scale of a bar graph increase by the same amount.
   Describe the scale on each bar graph.

a)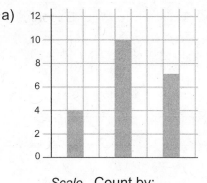

b)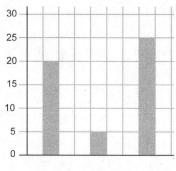

c)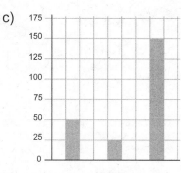

Scale Count by: _____

Stop at: _____

Scale Count by: _____

Stop at: _____

Scale Count by: _____

Stop at: _____

2.

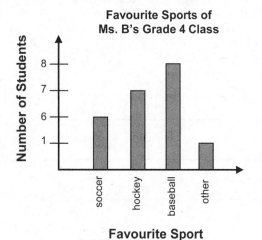

soccer	hockey	baseball	other
卌 |	卌 ||	卌 |||	|

a) How does the graph make it look like twice as many students chose baseball over soccer?
   HINT: Look at the height of each bar.

b) What is wrong with the scale?

c) Redraw the bar graph with the correct scale.

3. Choose a scale (that doesn't have too many or too few markings) and draw a bar graph for each set of data.

a)

Favourite Pizza Toppings	Pepperoni	Cheese	Mushrooms	Other
Number of People	20	15	18	3

b)

Math Score Range	1 – 5	6 – 10	11 – 15	16 – 20
Number of Students	2	8	35	5

4. Determine the values of the other bars on the graphs.

a)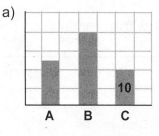

b)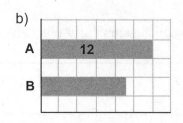

c)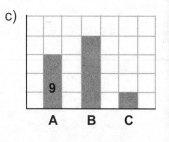

PDM4-9: Double Bar Graphs

A **double bar graph** compares two categories. Like a bar graph, it has a title, labels, a scale and vertical and horizontal axes. It also has a key showing what each type of bar means.

1.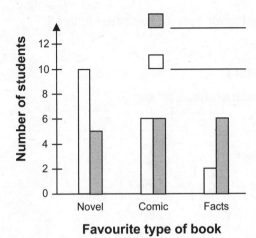

Favourite type of book	Novel	Comic	Facts
Girls	10	6	2
Boys	5	6	6

a) Fill in the key to show which bars represent boys and which represent girls.

b) What is the most popular type of book among girls?

_____

Overall? _____

c) Which type of book did the same number of boys and girls prefer?

_____

d) How many types of books are more popular with boys? _____

e) How many girls voted altogether? _____ Boys? _____

2. Kazuyo started drawing a double bar graph for the data below.
   She started with the summer data and drew her scale as shown.

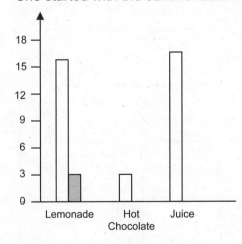

Favourite drink	Lemonade	Hot Chocolate	Juice
Summer	16	3	17
Winter	3	25	8

How does her scale make it hard to show the winter data?

Explain.

3. What scale would you choose for the given data?

Favourite Dessert	Ice Cream	Hot Apple Pie	Fruit Salad
Summer	40	2	8
Winter	5	22	23

What would you count by and where would the scale stop?

1. Do you think people would know the answer to each question?

    a) What's your favourite colour? _____

    b) On what day of the week were you born? _____

    c) When is your birthday? _____

    d) What's your eyeglasses prescription? _____

2. Data you collect yourself is called **primary** (or **first-hand**) data.

    Data collected by someone else is called **secondary** (or **second-hand**) data.

    How would you collect primary data for each question below?

    Choices: **A.** survey   **B.** observation   **C.** measurement

    a) How does the temperature of a cup of heated water change over time? __C__

    b) What are my classmates' favourite movies? _____

    c) How far can the students in your class jump? _____

    d) How many students in your class have blond hair? _____

    e) Do you think it will rain in the next twenty minutes? _____

3. George conducted a survey of his friends' favourite sports.

    He created a bar graph to display his data.

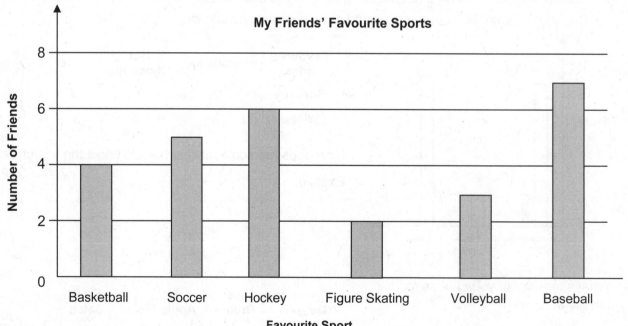

    a) Can you guess what George's tally sheet looked like? Try to recreate it.

    b) Instead of using a bar graph or tally sheet, how can George display his data?

Writing a Survey Question

The question should not have too many responses.
If appropriate, one of the responses could be "other."

FRUIT BAR

Example:

What is your favourite flavour of fruit bar?

✘ This question may give you too many answers.

What flavours of fruit bar do you like?
☐ apple ☐ grape ☐ strawberry ☐ other

✘ This question is not worded precisely. People could give more than one answer.

Which flavour of fruit bar is your favourite?
☐ apple ☐ grape ☐ strawberry ☐ other

✔ This <u>is</u> a better survey question. Each person will only give one answer.

✔ People will know the answer.

✔ People may choose other possibilities.

----

1. Add an "other" category if appropriate.
   HINT: If there are no other possibilities, don't add "other".

   a) What is your favourite sport?
      ☐ hockey ☐ volleyball ☐ basketball

   b) What is your favourite season?
      ☐ spring ☐ summer ☐ fall ☐ winter

   c) What is your favourite colour?
      ☐ blue ☐ red ☐ yellow

   d) What is your favourite primary colour?
      ☐ blue ☐ red ☐ yellow

2. Write a survey question to find out what pizza toppings students like best.

   _____

   _____ ?

   ☐ _____ ☐ _____ ☐ _____

   ☐ _____ ☐ _____ ☐ other?

3. Write a different survey question to ask your classmates.

jump math
MULTIPLYING POTENTIAL

4. Now it's your turn to design a survey.
   Record all of your ideas, data, observations and conclusions in your notebook.

Here are some suggestions to help you get started.

Step 1:
A survey asks a particular question, for example: How do you get to school? What is your favourite colour?
How big is your family?

Ask yourself:
What question will my survey ask?

Step 2:
You can give people a sample of possible answers, for instance: Do you walk to school or take the bus?

Ask yourself:
What are some of the responses I expect?

Step 3:
Try to predict the result. What answer do you think will be the most common? The least common?

Ask yourself:
What are my predicted results?

Step 4:
Make a tally sheet to keep track of the responses you receive. For example:

How do you get to school?	Tally
Walk	
Take the bus	
Ride my bike	

Step 5:
You'll need to display your data.

Ask yourself:
If I use a bar graph or a pictograph, what scale should I use?
If I use a pictograph, what symbol will work best? What will my key be?

Step 6:
Draw some conclusions about your original survey question.

Ask yourself:
Did people respond as I'd expected?
Were the results a surprise?
Did I learn anything interesting from my survey?

1. During the Olympics Games, Geoff kept track of the gold medals won by the following countries:

Korea	Italy	Greece	Brazil	Canada
⊮⊮ ⅠⅠⅠⅠ	⊮⊮ ⊮⊮	⊮⊮ Ⅰ	ⅠⅠⅠⅠ	ⅠⅠⅠ
9				

a) Complete the chart above.

b) How many gold medals did Brazil win? _____   c) How many did Greece win? _____

> You can **compare** and **order** data from the chart to find new information.

d) Which country won the __most__ gold medals? _____   e) the least? _____

> You can **add**, **subtract** or **multiply** data from the chart to find new information.

f) How many gold medals did the countries win altogether? _____

g) How many more medals did Italy win than Brazil? _____

h) Which country won three times as many gold medals as Canada? _____

2. Three students collected data and made graphs of their data.

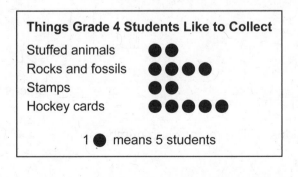

Things Grade 4 Students Like to Collect

Stuffed animals ●●
Rocks and fossils ●●●●
Stamps ●●●
Hockey cards ●●●●●

1 ● means 5 students

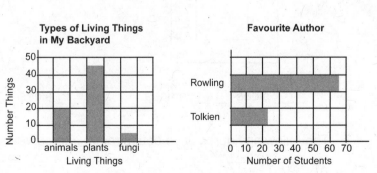

What information can you determine from each graph by comparing, ordering, adding, subtracting, multiplying, or dividing data amounts?

G4-1: Sides and Vertices of 2-D Figures

All polygons have **sides** (or 'edges') and
vertices (the 'corners' where the sides meet).

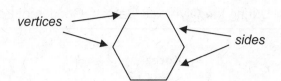

NOTE:
A polygon is a 2-D (flat) shape with sides that are straight lines.

---

1. Count the number of sides and vertices in each of the following figures. Put a check mark on each
    side and circle on each vertex as you count.

a)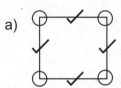

        __4__ sides

        __4__ vertices

b)

        ____ sides

        ____ vertices

c)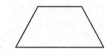

        ____ sides

        ____ vertices

d)

        ____ sides

        ____ vertices

e)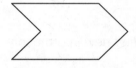

     ____ sides ____ vertices

f)

     ____ sides ____ vertices

g)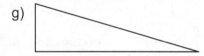

     ____ sides ____ vertices

BONUS

h)

     ____ sides ____ vertices

i)

     ____ sides ____ vertices

j)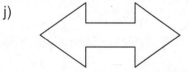

     ____ sides ____ vertices

k)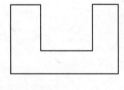

     ____ sides ____ vertices

l)

     ____ sides ____ vertices

m)

     ____ sides ____ vertices

2. The following figures have both straight and curved sides. Fill in the missing numbers.

a)

        _____ curved sides

        _____ straight sides

b)

        _____ curved sides

        _____ straight sides

Geometry 1

3. Helen names the shapes according to how many sides they have.

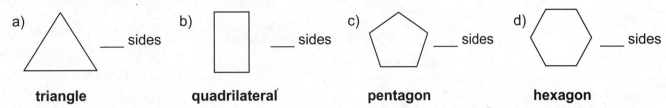

a) ___ sides   b) ___ sides   c) ___ sides   d) ___ sides

triangle   **quadrilateral**   **pentagon**   **hexagon**

4. Find the number of sides and complete the chart.

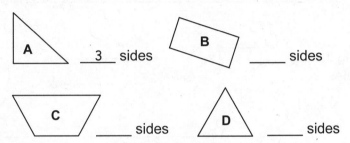

A __3__ sides   B ____ sides

C ____ sides   D ____ sides

Shapes	Letters
Triangles	A
Quadrilaterals	

5. Complete the chart. (Find as many shapes as you can for each shape name.)

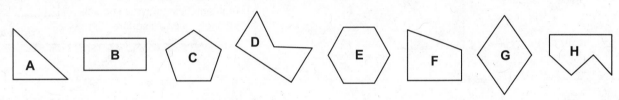

Shapes	Letters
Triangles	
Quadrilaterals	

Shapes	Letters
Pentagons	
Hexagons	

6. Using a ruler, draw a polygon with …
    a) 3 sides.
    b) 4 sides.

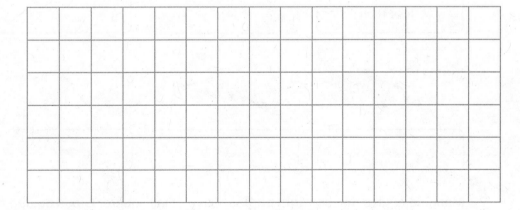

7. Draw a polygon with …   a) 5 sides.   b) 6 sides.

Can you draw a polygon in which the number of sides does not equal the number of vertices?

8. How many sides do two quadrilaterals and three pentagons have altogether?

G4-2: Introduction to Angles

An **angle** is formed when two lines intersect.

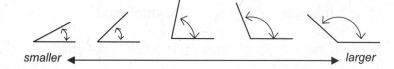

The lines that form an angle are called the arms.

vertex

The **size** of an angle measures the amount of rotation between the lines.

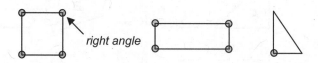

smaller ← → larger

RIGHT ANGLES

Right angles are found in many places, including the corners of squares, rectangles and some triangles.

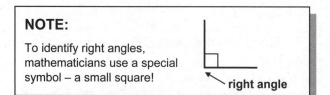

right angle

You can always check for right angles using the corner of a piece of paper.

piece of paper

right angle

NOTE:

To identify right angles, mathematicians use a special symbol – a small square!

right angle

---

1. Mark each angle as: (i) **less than** a right angle, or (ii) **greater than** a right angle.

    Check your answers with the corner of a piece of paper.

    a)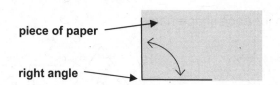

    | less than |

    b)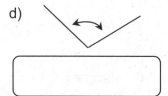

    c)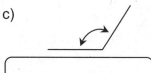

    d)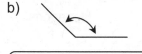

    e)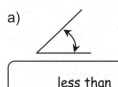

    f)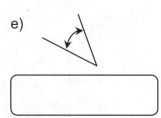

    g)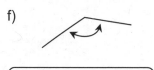

    h)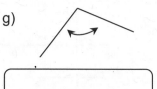

2. Mark the angles that are **right angles** with a small square. Cross out the angles that are not right angles.

    a)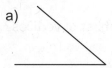

    b)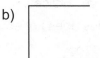

    c)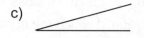

    d)

jump math MULTIPLYING POTENTIAL

Geometry 1

3. Draw two right angles, facing different directions and mark them properly with a small square.

Right Angle #1   **Right Angle #2**

4. Circle the figure that has no right angle.

5. Mark (with a small square) all the right angles in the following figures.
    Then circle the figures that have <u>two</u> right angles.

a)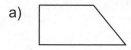

b)

c)

d)

e)

f)

6. a) Draw at least 3 letters of the alphabet that have at least one right angle.
        Mark all the right angles.

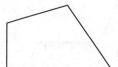

    b) Which letter of the alphabet do you think has the most right angles?

7. Angles that are less than a right angle are called **acute** angles.

    a) Draw at least 3 letters that have acute angles. Mark all the acute angles with dots.

    b) Can you find a letter that has both a right angle and an acute angle?

8. Angles that are greater than a right angle and less than two right angles are called **obtuse** angles.
    The letter A has 2 obtuse angles.
    Draw an A and mark the obtuse angles.

G4-3: Special Angles

1. Fold a piece of paper to create a half right angle.

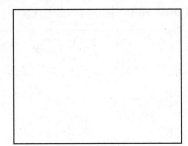

fold

half right angle

Circle the angles that are half right angles. (Use your half right angle to check.)

a)

b)

c)

d)

2.

In this house, mark 2 half right angles with:  and 5 right angles with: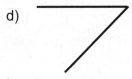

3. Using a ruler, divide each right angle into two half right angles.

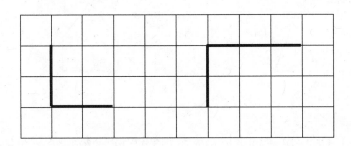

4. Mark any half right angles with: 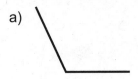 and any right angles with: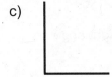

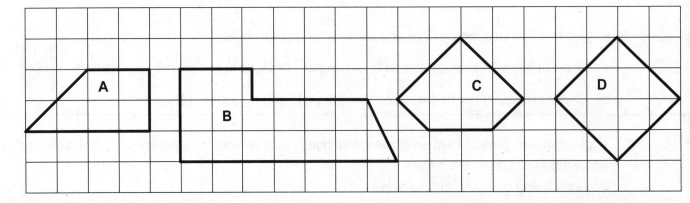

A

B

C

D

jump math
MULTIPLYING POTENTIAL

Geometry 1

G4-4: Measuring Angles

To measure an angle, you use a **protractor**. A protractor has 180 subdivisions around its circumference. The subdivisions are called degrees. 45° is a short form for "forty-five degrees."

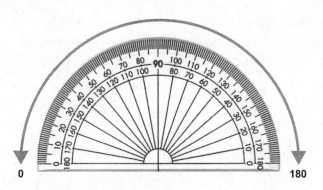

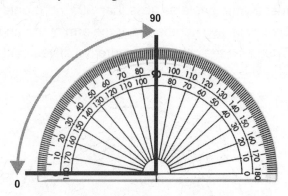

There are 180 subdivisions (180°) around the outside of a protractor.

There are 90° in a right angle (or a square corner).

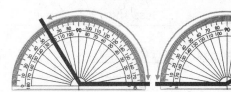

An angle can be less than 90° ...

... or greater than 90°.

----

1. Without using a protractor, identify each angle as "less than 90°" or "greater than 90°".

a)

_____

b)

_____

c)

_____

d)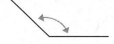

_____

e)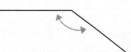

_____

f)

_____

g)

_____

h)

_____

i)

_____

G4-4: Measuring Angles (continued)

A protractor has two scales. The exercise below will help you decide which scale to use.

2. Identify the angle as "less than 90°" or "greater than 90°."
    Circle the <u>two</u> numbers that the arm of the angle passes through.
    Then pick the correct measure (i.e. if you said the angle is "less than 90°," pick the number that is less than 90).

a)

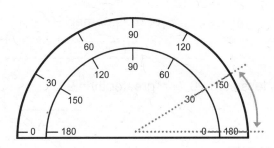

The angle is: _____less than 90°_____

The angle is: _____60°_____

b)

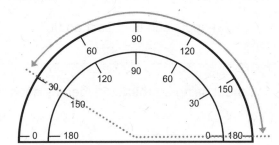

The angle is: _____

The angle is: _____

c)

The angle is: _____

The angle is: _____

d)

The angle is: _____

The angle is: _____

3. Again, identify the angle as "less than 90°" or "greater than 90°." Then write the measure of the angle.
    TEACHER: The letters beside each protractor are for a game in the Teacher's Guide.

a)   E

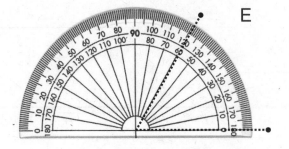

_____

b)   N

_____

MULTIPLYING POTENTIAL.

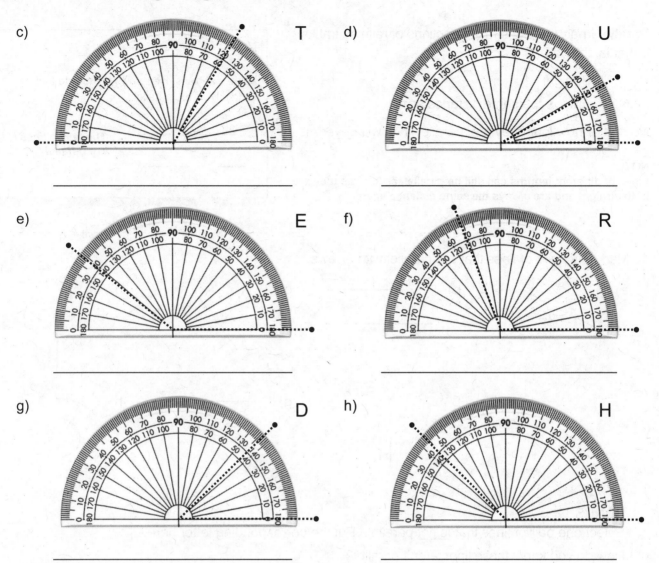

c) T

d) U

e) E

f) R

g) D

h) H

4. Measure the angles using a protractor, and write your answers in the boxes.

    HINT: Use a ruler to extend the arms in d), e) and f)

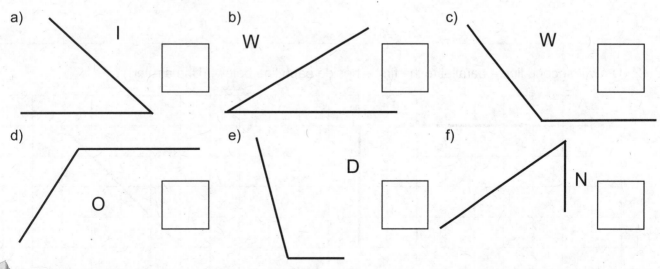

a) I

b) W

c) W

d) O

e) D

f) N

5. Draw 5 angles and use a protractor to measure them.

jump math
MULTIPLYING POTENTIAL.

Geometry 1

G4-5: Parallel Lines

Parallel lines are like straight sections of railway tracks
– that is, they are:

    ✓ Straight

    ✓ Always the same distance apart

No matter how long they are, parallel lines will <u>never</u> meet.

NOTE:
Lines of different lengths can still be parallel, as long as they are both straight and are always the same distance apart.

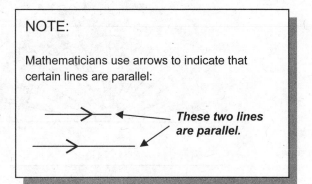

NOTE:

Mathematicians use arrows to indicate that certain lines are parallel:

These two lines are parallel.

---

1. Mark any pairs of lines that are parallel with arrows.

   a)    b) 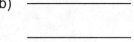   c)   d)

   e)   f)   g) 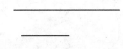   h)

BONUS

Select one pair of lines that <u>is not</u> parallel. Put the corresponding letter here - ⬚

How do you know these lines aren't parallel?

2. Draw a second line – parallel to the first – beside each line below. (Use a ruler!)

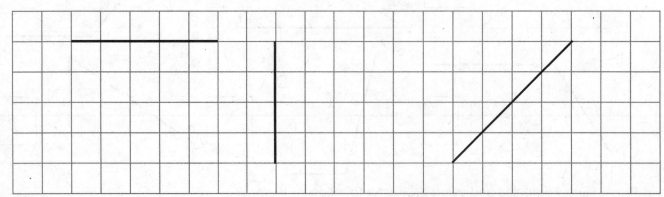

Geometry 1

3. The following pairs of lines are parallel. For each, join the dots to make a 4-sided figure. The first one has been done for you.

a)    b)   c)   d)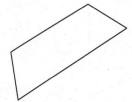

In each case, are the original two lines still parallel? _____

4. Each of the shapes below has **one pair** of parallel sides. Mark opposite sides that are <u>NOT parallel</u> with an 'X'. The first one has been done for you.

a)    b)   c)

d) 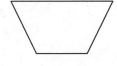   e) 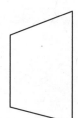   f) 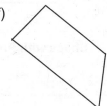   g)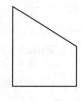

NOTE:

If a figure contains <u>more than a single pair</u> of parallel lines, you can avoid confusion by using a different number of arrows to mark each pair:

Example: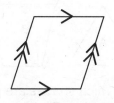

5. Using arrows, mark all the pairs of parallel lines in the figures below.

a)   b)   c) 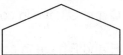   d)

____ pairs   ____ pair   ____ pairs   ____ pairs

G4-6: Quadrilaterals

A polygon with four sides is called a **quadrilateral**.

Example:

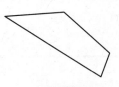

| 3 sides | 4 sides | 4 sides | 4 sides |
| NOT a quadrilateral | **quadrilateral** | **quadrilateral** | **quadrilateral** |

---

1. Based on the properties of the following figures, complete the chart below.

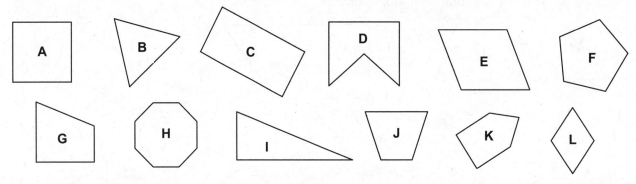

Property	Shape with Property
Quadrilateral	
Non-Quadrilateral	

2.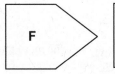

a) Which shapes are polygons? **REMEMBER: A polygon has straight sides.** _____

b) Which shapes have sides that are all the same length? (Check with a ruler.) _____

c) Which shapes have at least one curved side? _____

d) What do shapes B, C and G have in common? _____

e) What do shapes D, E and F have in common? _____

f) Which shape doesn't belong in this group: A, E, F and G? Explain. _____

g) Pick your own group of shapes and say what they have in common. _____

_____

G4-7: Properties of Shapes

Some quadrilaterals don't have any pairs of parallel lines. Some have one pair of parallel lines. Parallelograms have **two** pairs of parallel lines.

 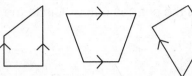 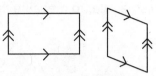

NO parallel lines   **ONE** pair of parallel lines   **TWO** pairs of parallel lines

----

1. For each shape, mark the parallel lines with arrows. Mark all of the opposite sides that are not parallel with an 'X'. Under each quadrilateral, write how many <u>pairs</u> of sides are parallel.

A _____   B _____   C _____   D _____

   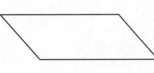   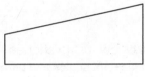   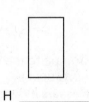

E _____   F _____   G _____   H _____

2. Sort the above shapes into the chart by writing the letter in the correct column.

No pairs of parallel sides	One pair of parallel sides	Two pairs of parallel sides

3. Using the figures below, complete the two charts. Start by marking the right angles and parallel lines in each figure.

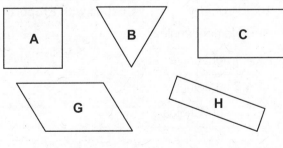 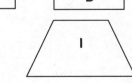 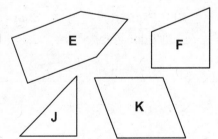

a)

Property	Shapes with Property
No right angles	
1 right angle	
2 right angles	
4 right angles	

b)

Property	Shapes with Property
No parallel lines	
1 pair	
2 pairs	

MULTIPLYING POTENTIAL

Geometry 1

NOTE: A shape with all sides the same length is called <u>equilateral</u>. ("Equi" comes from a Latin word meaning "equal" and "lateral" means "sides".)

4. Use a ruler to measure the sides of the shapes below. Circle the shapes that are equilateral.

a)

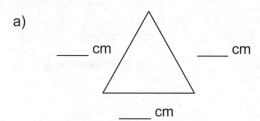

____ cm ____ cm

____ cm

b)

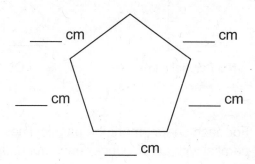

____ cm ____ cm

____ cm ____ cm

____ cm

c)

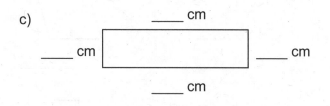

____ cm

____ cm ____ cm

____ cm

d)

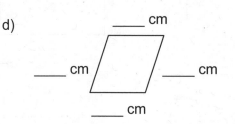

____ cm

____ cm ____ cm

____ cm

5. Complete the charts below, using shapes A to J for <u>each chart</u>.

HINT: Start by marking the right angles and parallel lines in each figure. If you are not sure if a figure is equilateral, measure its sides with a ruler.

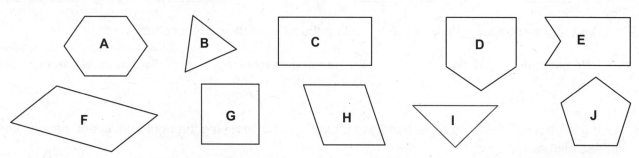

a)

Property	Shapes with Property
Equilateral	
Not equilateral	

b)

Property	Shapes with Property
No right angles	
1 right angle	
2 right angles	
4 right angles	

c)

Property	Shapes with Property
No parallel sides	
1 pair of parallel sides	
2 pairs of parallel sides	
3 pairs of parallel sides	

d)

Shape Names	Shapes
Triangles	
Quadrilaterals	
Pentagons	
Hexagons	

G4-8: Special Quadrilaterals

A quadrilateral (shape with 4 sides) with two pairs of parallel sides is called a **parallelogram**.

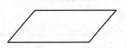

Parallelogram
A quadrilateral with two pairs of parallel sides.

Some other quadrilaterals have special names.

   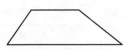

Rhombus
A parallelogram with 4 equal sides

Rectangle
A parallelogram with 4 right-angles

Square
A parallelogram with 4 right-angles and 4 equal sides

Trapezoid
A quadrilateral with only one pair of parallel sides

----

1. Mark all right angles in the quadrilaterals and measure the length of each side.
   Then chose the best (or most specific) name for each quadrilateral.

   a)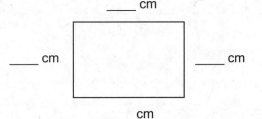
   ____ cm
   ____ cm
   ____ cm
   ____ cm

   Name: _____

   b)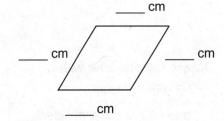
   ____ cm
   ____ cm
   ____ cm
   ____ cm

   Name: _____

2. Name the shapes. Use the words rhombus, square, parallelogram and rectangle.

   a)    b)    c)   d)

3. Mark all the right angles in each quadrilateral. Then identify each quadrilateral.

   a)    b)   c)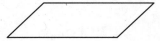

   _____   _____   _____

4. Match the name of the quadrilateral to the best description.

Square	A parallelogram with 4 right angles.
Rectangle	A parallelogram with 4 equal sides.
Rhombus	A parallelogram with 4 right angles and 4 equal sides.

Geometry 1

5. For each quadrilateral, write how many <u>pairs</u> of sides are parallel. Then identify each quadrilateral.

a)

b)

c)

_____   _____   _____

_____   _____   _____

6. Draw a quadrilateral with …
    a) no right angle.
    b) one right angle.
    c) two right angles.

7. Draw a quadrilateral with …
    a) no parallel sides.
    b) one pair of parallel sides.
    c) two pairs of parallel sides and no right angles.

8. Use the words "all", "some", or "no" for each statement.

    a) _____ squares are rectangles.   b) _____ trapezoids are parallelograms.

    c) _____ parallelograms are trapezoids.   d) _____ parallelograms are rectangles.

9. If a shape has four right angles, which two special quadrilaterals might it be?

10. If a quadrilateral has all equal sides, which two special quadrilaterals might it be?

11. Write three different names for a square.

12. Describe any similarities or differences between …
    a) a rhombus and a parallelogram.   b) a rhombus and a square.
    c) a trapezoid and a parallelogram.

G4-9: Tangrams

A **tangram** is an ancient Chinese puzzle.

The tangram is a square divided into seven pieces called **tans**.

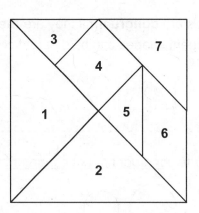

TEACHER:
Your students will need a copy of the larger tangram in the Teacher's Guide. Students may need your help cutting out the shapes. (It is important that the shapes are cut accurately.)

---

1. Which tans are …

    a) quadrilaterals? _____

    b) triangles? _____

    c) parallelograms? _____

2. You can make a square and a rectangle using tans.

    Make a <u>square</u> using …

    a) tans 1 and 2.

    b) tans 3, 5 and 7.

    c) tans 1, 3, 4, and 5

    Make a <u>rectangle</u> using …

    d) tans 3, 4 and 5.

    e) tans 1, 3, 5 and 7.

    NOTE: Trace around your tans to show how you made each figure.

3. Predict the shapes you can make using the tans listed in the chart below (look for triangles, quadrilaterals, pentagons, hexagons, trapezoids and parallelograms).

Tan Pieces	Predicted Shapes	Shapes Made
5, 6		
3, 5, 6		
3, 5, 6, 7		

Shapes are **congruent** if they are **the same size and shape**.
Congruent shapes can be different colours and shades. These pairs of shapes are congruent:

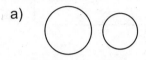 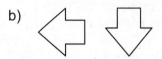 

---

1. Write <u>congruent</u> or <u>not congruent</u> under each pair of shapes.

   a)   b)   c)

       <u>Not congruent</u>

2. Circle the pairs of shapes that are congruent.

   a)    b)

   c)    d)

   e)    f)

   g)    h)

   i)    j)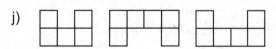

3. Label congruent shapes with the same letter pair. **HINT: You will need the letters A and B.**

4. Draw a shape that is congruent to each shape below.

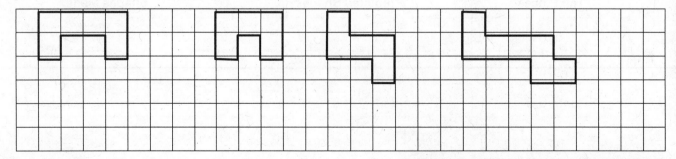

G4-11: Congruency (Advanced)

1. Draw a second shape that covers the same number of squares but is NOT congruent.

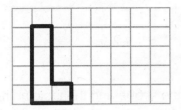

2. Draw a second figure that is the same shape as the one below but is NOT congruent.

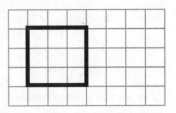

3. Label any congruent shapes with the same letter.
   HINT: You will need to use the letters A, B, C and D.

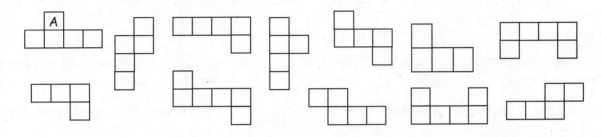

4. Shade regions in the right-hand grid to make the two figures congruent.

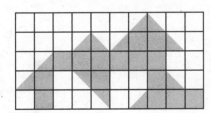

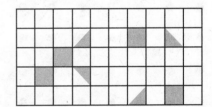

5. Are these pairs of shapes congruent?

   a) _____ because _____.

   b) _____ because _____.

BONUS
6. Add …

   a) 2 lines to make 3 congruent squares.

   b) 3 lines to make 4 congruent triangles.

   c) 2 lines to make 3 congruent rectangles.

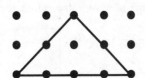

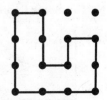

7. Find two congruent shapes in your classroom. How can you check that they are congruent?

Some shapes have lines of **symmetry**. Tina places a mirror across half the shape. If the half reflected in the mirror makes her picture whole again, the shape is symmetrical.

 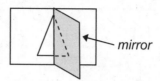

mirror

Tina also checks if a shape has a line of symmetry by cutting out the shape and then folding it. If the halves of the shapes on either side of the fold match exactly, Tina knows that the fold shows a **line of symmetry**.

---

1. Complete the picture so it has a <u>horizontal</u> line of symmetry.

   Then draw in the line of symmetry.

   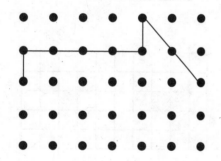

2. Complete the picture so it has a <u>vertical</u> line of symmetry.

   Then draw in the line of symmetry.

   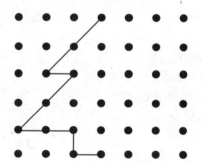

3. Using a ruler, draw a <u>horizontal</u> line of symmetry through each figure.

   a)    b)

4. Draw a <u>vertical</u> line of symmetry through each figure.

   a)   b)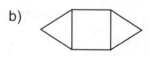

5. Draw horizontal <u>and/or</u> vertical lines of symmetry in the following figures.
   NOTE: Some figures may have both lines of symmetry, while some may have neither.

   a)   b) 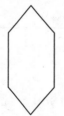   c)   d) 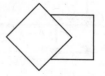   e)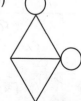

G4-13: Symmetry and Paper Folding

1. Cut out copies of the shapes shown below.

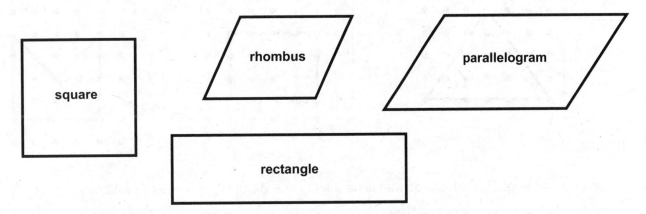

a) Predict how many lines of symmetry each shape will have. Write the answer in the chart.

b) Fold your shapes to check how many lines of symmetry they have.

Draw the lines of symmetry onto the shapes above.

Then complete the chart.

Shape	Predicted number of lines of symmetry	Actual number of lines of symmetry
Square		
Rectangle		
Rhombus		
Parallelogram		

2. Cut out copies of the shapes shown below. Find all the lines of symmetry for each shape.

NOTE: "Regular" means "equilateral" and having equal angles.

 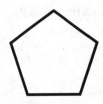 

Equilateral Triangle   Square   Regular Pentagon   Regular Hexagon

a)

Figure	Triangle	Square	Pentagon	Hexagon
Number of edges				
Number of lines of symmetry				

b) Describe any relation you see between the number of lines of symmetry and the number of edges of a regular polygon.

G4-14: More Symmetry

1. Draw a line of symmetry through each shape, parallel to line A.

a)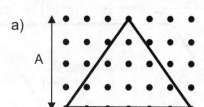

b)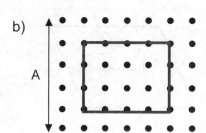

c)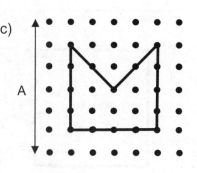

2. Draw a line through each shape that is parallel to line B but is <u>not</u> a line of symmetry.

a)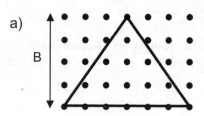

b)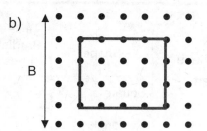

c)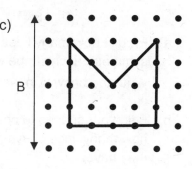

3. Many letters of the alphabet have lines of symmetry.

a) Draw at least 5 letters of the alphabet and show their lines of symmetry.

b) Can you find a letter with 2 or more lines of symmetry?

4. Decode the words written in "mirror code" by filling in the missing half of each letter.

a)   b)   c)

G4-15: Triangles

Triangles can be classified by the lengths of their sides.

   i)   All three sides of an **equilateral triangle** are of equal length.

   ii)   Two sides of an **isosceles triangle** are of equal length.

   iii)   No two sides of a **scalene triangle** are of equal length.

---

1. a) Measure the sides of each triangle. Write your measurements on the sides.

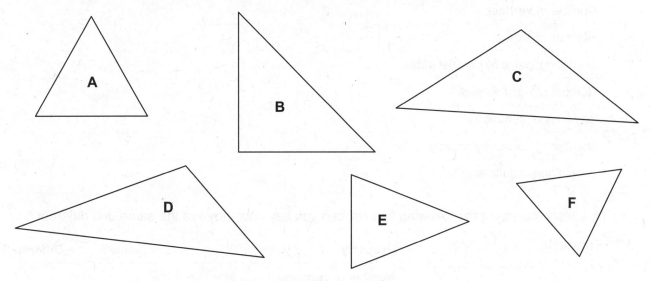

   b) Classify the triangles by their sides.

Property	Triangles with Property
Equilateral	
Isosceles	
Scalene	

2. Measure the following lines and then mark the midpoint of each.

   a) _____ _____ cm   b) _____ _____ cm

3. Each of the triangles below is isosceles.
   Draw the line of symmetry for each.
   HINT: First find the midpoint of the base as in triangle A.

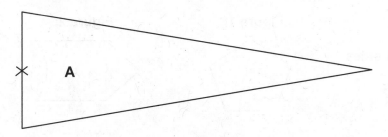

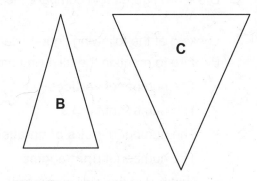

1.

Figure 1:   Figure 2: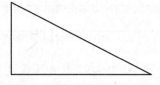

a) Compare the two shapes by completing the following chart.

Property	Figure 1	Figure 2	Same?	Different?
Number of **vertices**	3	3	✓	
Number of **edges**				
Number of **pairs of parallel sides**				
Number of **right angles**				
Any lines of **symmetry**?				
Number of lines of **symmetry**				
Is the figure **equilateral**?				

b) By simply looking at the following figures, can you say how they are the same and different?

Figure 1:

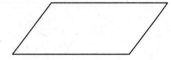

Figure 2:

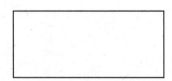

Property	Same?	Different?
Number of **vertices**		
Number of **edges**		
Number of **pairs of parallel sides**		
Number of **right angles**		
Any lines of **symmetry**?		
Number of lines of **symmetry**		
Is the figure **equilateral**?		

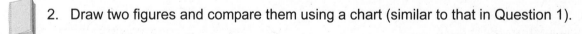

2. Draw two figures and compare them using a chart (similar to that in Question 1).

3. Looking at the following figures, can you comment on their <u>similarities</u> and <u>differences</u>?
    Be sure to mention the following properties:

    ✓ The number of **vertices**
    ✓ The number of **edges**
    ✓ The number of **pairs of parallel sides**
    ✓ The number of **right angles**
    ✓ Number of **lines of symmetry**
    ✓ Are the figures **equilateral**?

Figure 1:   Figure 2:

1. The following figures can be sorted by their properties using a Venn diagram.

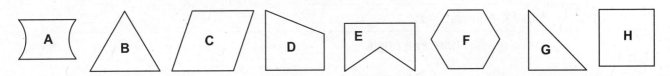

a)

Property:	Figures with this property:
1. I am a quadrilateral	C, D, H
2. I have at least 2 right angles	D, E, H

Which figures share both properties? _____

Using the information in the chart above, complete the following Venn diagram.

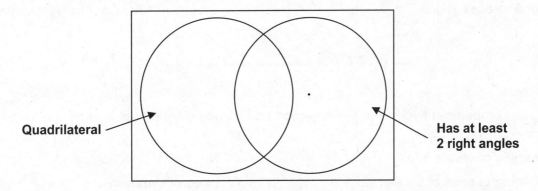

Quadrilateral

Has at least 2 right angles

Using figures A through H above, complete the charts and the Venn diagrams below.

b)

Property:	Figures with this property:
1. I am a quadrilateral	
2. All of my sides are the same length	

Which figures share both properties? _____

Using the information in the chart above, complete the following Venn diagram.

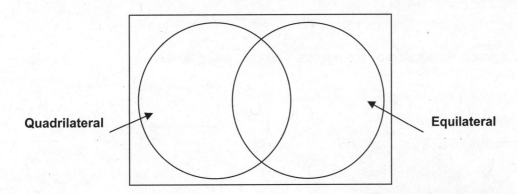

Quadrilateral

Equilateral

c)

Property:	Figures with this property:
1. I have 4 or 5 vertices	
2. I have at least one right angle	

Which figures share both properties? _____

Using the information in the chart above, complete the following Venn diagram.

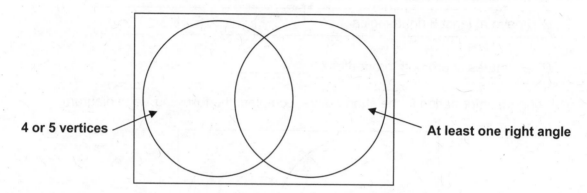

4 or 5 vertices   **At least one right angle**

2. Using two properties of your own make a chart and a Venn diagram (as in Question 1). You may choose from the following:

✓ Number of vertices   ✓ Number of right angles

✓ Number of pairs of parallel sides   ✓ Lines of symmetry

✓ Number of edges   ✓ Equilateral

3. Describe each figure completely. Your description should mention the following properties:

✓ Number of sides   ✓ Number of right angles

✓ Number of vertices   ✓ Number of lines of symmetry

✓ Number of pairs of parallel sides   ✓ Is the figure equilateral?

a) 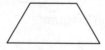   b)    c)

4. List all the properties shared by the figures. Then list any differences.

a)   b)

G4-18: Sorting and Classifying Shapes (Review)

1. Record the properties of each shape by writing "yes" or "no" in the corresponding columns.

 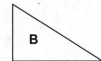 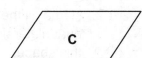

Shape	Quadrilateral	Equilateral	Two pairs of Parallel Sides	At least one Right Angle
A				
B				
C				
D				
E				

2. Count the vertices and edges in the figures. Mark right angles with a square. Mark pairs of parallel sides with arrows. Write T (for true) if the figures share the property. Otherwise, write F (for false).

Both figures have...

a)

____ 4 vertices   ____ 2 pairs of parallel sides

____ 4 sides   ____ 2 right angles

b)

____ 3 vertices   ____ 5 sides

____ no right angles   ____ equilateral

c)

____ quadrilateral   ____ 2 pairs of parallel sides

____ at least one right angle

d)

____ 6 vertices   ____ no right angles

____ at least 2 pairs of parallel sides

3. Name the shapes based on the descriptions.

a) I have three sides. All of my sides are the same length. I'm an _____.

b) I have four equal sides. None of my angles are right angles. I'm a _____.

c) I am a quadrilateral with two pairs of parallel sides. I'm a _____.

1. How many right angles are there in this figure?

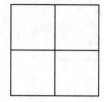

2. Name all the quadrilaterals in this shape.

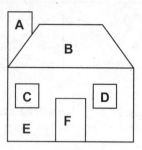

3. Which of the quadrilaterals have only one name? Two names? Three names? Write as many names as you can for each figure.

 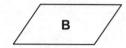 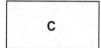 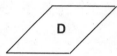 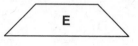

4. Which of these shapes are congruent? Explain.

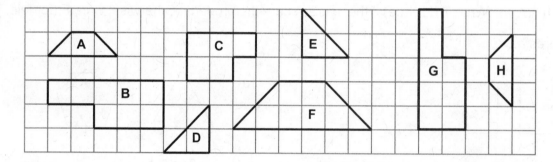

5.

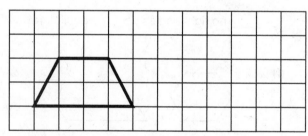

The shape on the grid is a <u>trapezoid</u>.

a) On the grid, draw a second trapezoid that has 2 right angles. Mark the right angles.

b) How do you know both shapes are trapezoids?

6. a) Why is a square a rectangle?　　b) Why is a rectangle not always a square?

c) Why is a trapezoid not a parallelogram?

7. a) I have 4 equal sides, but no right angles. What am I?

b) I have 4 right angles, but my sides are not all equal. What am I?

BONUS

c) I have exactly 2 right angles. Which special quadrilateral <u>could</u> I be?